always up to date

The law changes, but Nolo is on top of it! We offer several
ways to make sure you and your Nolo products are up to date:

1 **Nolo's Legal Updater**
We'll send you an email whenever a new edition of this book
is published! Sign up at **www.nolo.com/legalupdater**.

2 **Updates @ Nolo.com**
Check www.nolo.com/update to find recent changes
in the law that affect the current edition of your book.

3 **Nolo Customer Service**
To make sure that this edition of the book is the most
recent one, call us at **800-728-3555** and ask one of
our friendly customer service representatives.
Or find out at **www.nolo.com**.

please note

We believe accurate, plain-English legal information should help you solve many of your own legal problems. But this text is not a substitute for personalized advice from a knowledgeable lawyer. If you want the help of a trained professional—and we'll always point out situations in which we think that's a good idea—consult an attorney licensed to practice in your state.

7th edition

Deeds for California Real Estate

by Mary Randolph, J.D.

NOLO

SEVENTH EDITION   JANUARY 2007

Book Design   TERRI HEARSH

Illustration   MARI STEIN

Proofreading   ROBERT WELLS

Index   BAYSIDE INDEXING SERVICE

Cover Photography   TONYA PERME (www.tonyaperme.com)

Printing   CONSOLIDATED PRINTERS, INC.

Randolph, Mary.
    Deeds for California real estate / by Mary Randolph.-- 7th ed.
    p. cm.
    ISBN 1-4133-0621-7 (alk. paper)
    1. Deeds--California--Popular works. 2. Land titles--Registration and transfer--California--Popular works. I
Title.
KFC170.Z9R36 2006
346.79404'38--dc22   2006046799

For information on bulk purchases or corporate premium sales, please contact the Special Sales Department.
For academic sales or textbook adoptions, ask for Academic Sales. Call 800-955-4775 or write to Nolo, 950 Parker
Street, Berkeley, CA 94710.

Acknowledgments

My first thanks must go to Jake Warner and Steve Elias, who let themselves be talked into giving me a job at Nolo. When it comes to this book, it's trite but true: I couldn't have done it without them.

Sincere thanks also go to Jackie Mancuso, Keija Kimura, Amy Ihara, and Toni Ihara, who patiently designed the first edition of the book and wrestled with the computers until it came out right. Thanks to Terri Hearsh, who completely redesigned the book for its snappy fifth edition.

Real estate experts Ira Serkes, George Devine, and the late Hayden Curry, and financial expert Malcolm Roberts provided help along the way and commented helpfully on the manuscript. Attorney Katherine Stoner also helped with community property issues.

And thanks to my parents, who gave me genes for writing and law.

Table of Contents

Your Real Estate Companion

1 An Overview of Real Property Transfers

2 Who Must Sign the Deed?

3 How Should the New Owners Take Title?

4 Deeds of Trust

5 Preparing Your Deed

6 Recording Your Deed

7 When You Need an Expert

Glossary

Appendix

Index

Your Real Estate Companion

Every time you change who owns real estate, or change how you own it, you need to prepare and file a new deed. But where do you get the right deed form? Will transferring property trigger a property tax reassessment? Will you owe gift tax? Where do you file the deed?

This book answers those questions and more. It shows you how to transfer or mortgage title to almost any kind of California real estate, including houses, undeveloped land, farms, commercial buildings, and condos.

It provides the forms and instructions you need to make these (and other) common kinds of transactions:

- **Put real estate into a living trust.** If you've made a living trust to avoid probate, good for you. But the most common mistake people make when they create trusts is forgetting to actually transfer their property into the trustee's name. And if you don't do that, your trust is worthless.

- **Add a co-owner to real estate.** Lots of older folks consider adding an adult child or other younger relative as a co-owner, to make passing ownership of the property easier. But there are potential problems with this approach, and usually better ways to achieve your goals. You'll learn the pros and cons.

- **Buy out one co-owner.** If you own real estate jointly with someone else, and one of you wants to buy out the other, you'll need a new deed.

- **Change the way you hold title to real estate.** Especially if you're married, you and your spouse want to be sure you're holding title to your house or other real estate in the most advantageous way.

Making these kinds of changes isn't usually difficult. You'll probably just have to fill out a deed form and file it at the county recorder's office. The book will show you how to pick the deed form you need, how to fill it out, and how to record it.

Along the way, we'll alert you to any potential complications: gift taxes, spouses' property rights, disclosure statements required by state or federal law, and due-on-sale clauses in loans. We'll also tell you when it would be wise to consult a lawyer, real estate agent, or tax specialist. (This book doesn't cover sales on the open market, out-of-state property, or removing the name of a deceased co-owner.) But it's unlikely that any of these issues will keep you from making the changes you want to make.

All this may seem a little confusing. But just follow the steps in the book, use the simple tear-out forms you'll find in the appendix, and you'll be on your way.

Chapter 1

An Overview of Real Property Transfers

Property transfers can have important legal and tax consequences. Before you start the paperwork, it pays to patiently go over the key issues, including property ownership, lender policies, title rules, tax implications of transfers, and California's real estate disclosure laws. You may even learn something that prompts you to change the way you make the transfer.

For example, here are some of the questions you should keep in mind:

- Will the transfer make loans on the property come due all at once?
- Will the property transfer you have in mind trigger a local property tax reassessment, causing an increase in the property tax?
- Will the transfer necessitate filing a gift tax return with the IRS?
- Are the current owners legally obligated to make written disclosures to the new owner about defects in the property?
- If you transfer property and then declare bankruptcy soon after, could creditors have the transfer invalidated?

The good news is that few of these issues are likely to apply to your situation. This chapter explains each issue; reading the first paragraph or two of each section should let you determine whether or not the material is relevant.

Understanding Basic Terminology

Before we go on, let's stop a minute and define a few important real estate terms. A much more complete glossary is in the back of the book.

Don't despair if it seems like a short course in Greek; we'll redefine the important terms when you run across them again.

Real Property

Real property (real estate) is land and things permanently attached to land—everything from houses and trees down to built-in appliances. Thus, a mobile home that is installed on a foundation is usually considered real property. Anything that's

Checklist for Real Property Transfers	
Current owner must:	**New owner must:**
Determine who must sign the deed	Decide whether or not to buy title insurance
If there are existing loans, check with lender to see if balance will become due when property sold	Order title search, if necessary
	Decide how to take title
Make disclosures about condition of property, if required by statute	
Fill out and sign correct deed form	
Have signatures on the deed notarized	
Deliver deed to new owner	
	Record deed with county recorder's office, pay transfer tax if applicable, and file Preliminary Change in Ownership Report with county recorder
File federal gift tax return, if necessary	
File IRS Form 2119 (*Sale of Your Home*) with the year's income tax return, if required	
	File Change in Ownership Statement with county assessor, if required

not real property is "personal property." Personal property that has been permanently attached to a structure on the property (for example, chandeliers or built-in bookshelves) is considered a "fixture" and part of the real property. It automatically passes to the new owner under a deed, unless the parties to the transfer agree otherwise.

Ownership

"Ownership" of real property, as a legal concept, is more complicated than it may appear. Most people think of ownership as an absolute thing—you either own property or you don't. The law, however, sees property ownership as a package of distinct "ownership interests." This package can be split in certain ways, and pieces of property ownership given to different people.

There are two common ways for ownership of property to be split. One is when ownership is shared at the same time. For instance, if you and your spouse, or you and your three sisters, own a house together, you each own part of the whole interest in the property. (Depending on how title to the property is held—as a joint tenancy, tenancy in common, community property, etc.—the co-owners have different legal rights and responsibilities. See Chapter 3.)

Other "interests" in property can also be shared at the same time. For example, a neighbor may own an easement—a legal right to use part of your land subject to certain conditions (for example, the right to run a water pipe or path over a certain part of the land). As an easement owner, the neighbor is in essence a "co-owner" (although he would never be referred to as such in normal conversation) and you must take his rights into consideration before you transfer the property. Put differently, you can only transfer what you own—and if a neighbor acquired part of your ownership rights in the form of a right-of-way across the land, there's nothing you can do about it now. When you transfer the land, the easement goes with it, and the new owner takes the property subject to the easement.

Someone with a lease on the property also has some of the rights of the owner—the right to possess the property during the term of the lease, of course, is the important one. He can transfer those rights (if the lease permits it). Similarly, the owner can transfer her ownership rights, but can't end or interfere with the rights of the person with the lease. In other words, the property is transferred subject to the lease.

Ownership can also be shared over time. For instance, a deed may specify that one person owns property only for a certain period of time (most frequently, his lifetime). If someone has such a "life estate," somebody else, by necessity, has an ownership interest in the property that will take effect after the first person dies. This second person's ownership rights do not include the right to use the property while the first owner is alive. But the second owner may, for instance, require the first owner to maintain the property's value by keeping it in good shape and making property tax and mortgage payments. These arrangements are quite rare these days. They are leftovers from the English feudal system of land ownership, when real property was almost the only measure of wealth and power and it was common for ownership interests to be divided intricately among many heirs.

When California Was a Bargain

How does $1.25 (or nothing) an acre for California land sound? Unfortunately, you're a century and a half too late.

When the United States acquired California at the end of the Mexican-American War in 1848, it promised to respect the rights of landowners who had obtained title from the Mexican government. Everything else went to the United States government. A few years later, after California was admitted to the Union in 1850, federal law allowed settlers to squat on public land and then buy it for $1.25 an acre. The 1862 Homestead Act went even further, giving up to 160 acres to a settler who lived on it and cultivated it for five years.

Title

The owner of a piece of property is said to have "title" to it. Title is proof of ownership. In that sense, title is just a shorthand way of referring to ownership. However, the two terms are not synonymous. It is possible to change the title—the way in which property is owned—without changing who owns it. For instance, if before you married, you and your current spouse took title to property as tenants in common, you might now want to change it so that title is held as community property. You would continue to own the property together, but the change in the way you hold title would produce a different set of consequences when you or your spouse died. We discuss these kinds of transfers in more detail in Chapter 3.

Title Search

To find out who owns property and how they hold the title to it, the first step is to look at the deed, which shows the current owners. Deeds, however, do not reveal certain kinds of problems with title to property. To confirm ownership requires a title search—a search of all public records of the property. Usually done by a title insurance company, the search includes examining copies of all the deeds that have ever transferred it, easements granted over it, liens placed against it, and tax and court records.

Checking the public records is usually reliable because all ownership interests in land are supposed to be recorded with the county to be fully effective (the recording system is discussed in Chapter 6). All deeds passing the property from owner to owner should be on record.

Evidence of other interests in the land will most likely be in the form of a document granting an easement, giving the property as security for a loan, or announcing that someone has placed a lien on the property to insure payment of a debt or taxes.

Title searches are routine whenever property is transferred and a bank or savings and loan is involved. Before making a loan that is secured by the property, a lender wants to make sure that the buyer is getting good title to it. Title searches are not necessary in some intrafamily transfers or when owners just want to change the way they hold title.

Title Insurance

Title companies guarantee the results of their searches by issuing title insurance policies, usually in the amount of the value of the property. Title insurance protects an owner (or whoever loaned money to finance the purchase of the property) against losses that result from a defect in the title that exists when the policy is issued and is discovered later. For example, a typical title insurance policy would cover an owner's losses if any of the transfer documents are fraudulent or forged, or if there is a lien or easement on the property that the title company didn't find when it searched the records. If an owner puts in a claim under the policy, the insurance company can, like any other insurance company, defend the owner in a lawsuit or negotiate a settlement.

In many private, intrafamily transfers, where no institutional lender is financing the purchase and all the parties are confident that the title is clear, they decide not to buy title insurance. In many situations, however, title insurance is a wise investment. Title insurance, and how to get it if you decide you want it, are discussed below.

Deeds

Deeds are the documents that transfer ownership of real property. In California, the most common kinds are grant, quitclaim, and trust deeds. Their functions are quite different. Here is a very brief overview of each:

Grant deed: The most commonly used type of deed. It contains guarantees that title being passed hasn't already been transferred to someone else or been encumbered (see the next section), except as specified in the deed. The grantor is the person transferring the property; the grantee is the person receiving it.

Quitclaim deed: A deed that is used to give up one's claims to land. Unlike a grant deed, the quitclaim deed makes no promises about the title being transferred. The maker of a quitclaim deed simply transfers whatever interest in the land he may have at the time. Quitclaims are often used when someone has a theoretical claim to real property; the potential claimant gives up the claim, and the property's owner doesn't have to worry about the claim being made later. They can also be used instead of a grant deed; they are just as effective to transfer ownership of property.

Trust deed (deed of trust): A trust deed isn't used to transfer ownership of property. It comes into play when someone uses real property as security for a loan—which is almost anytime someone buys real estate. It is used in conjunction with a promissory note (a written promise to pay back a loan). The buyer signs the note and a trust deed, which permits its holder (the trustee) to sell the property and pay off the loan if the buyer defaults.

Encumbrance

An encumbrance is any legal claim on property that affects an owner's ability to transfer title to the property. Common encumbrances are deeds of trust, mortgages, and past-due property tax liens (claims filed against the property when property taxes are delinquent). If your property is encumbered—say, for example, there is a trust deed on the property because you borrowed money to buy it—before you can transfer title you will either have to remove the encumbrance (by paying off the loan secured by the trust deed) or get the buyer to agree to take the property subject to the encumbrance. (In the case of a trust deed, you would most likely also have to get the approval of the lender for the new owner to take over the loan.)

Encumbrances

If, like most homeowners, you borrowed money to buy your house and signed a deed of trust securing the loan, title to the property is encumbered. Past-due property taxes are another fairly common encumbrance. But you can skip this discussion if:

- the property being transferred has no existing deeds of trust, mortgages, past-due property taxes, or homeowners' association assessments, liens, or other encumbrances on its title (for example, the property is owned outright, free of ownership or lien claims by others, and property tax payments are up-to-date), or
- the owner(s) want only to change the form in which title is held (for example, from tenancy in common to joint tenancy, or from a single owner to a revocable trust with the owner as trustee), and the identity of the owners doesn't change.

If money is changing hands for the property, or a new owner is involved, or if you really don't know for sure whether or not there are encumbrances, it is wise to investigate just how clear the transferor's title to the property really is. That's when you need a title search (discussed later in this chapter).

Deeds and Encumbrances

When you use a grant deed (the kind of deed used most often in California) to transfer property, you automatically promise that you have disclosed to the new owner all encumbrances you have incurred. (Civil Code § 1113.) If you do not disclose the existence of such an encumbrance, you can be liable for the new owner's damages. For example, if you neglect to tell the buyer that there is a huge tax lien on the property, the buyer can sue you for what it costs to pay off the lien.

Under the law, the encumbrances about which a grantor must tell the grantee, when transferring property with a grant deed, include taxes, assessments, and liens on the property. (Civil Code § 1114.)

For example, if a carpenter who worked on a house has recorded a mechanic's lien on the property to insure that he is paid, the grantor must disclose it. Otherwise a recipient would take title to the property subject to the lien.

You are not promising that you have good title to the property. You are not responsible for other claims on the property that aren't based on your acts and are out of your control. The most common examples of such claims (none of them is very common) are claims by someone whose claim arose under a former owner, and eminent domain (condemnation) proceedings by government entities. For example, if you receive a grant deed to property and then find out there are condemnation proceedings underway, you're out of luck as far as suing under the promise that the statute says is implied in the grant deed.

Because buyers (and lenders) do not usually want to rely on the seller's disclosure and implied promise, they routinely order title searches and purchase title insurance. If a problem with the title (including an encumbrance that they didn't know about when they bought) is discovered later, the insurance will pay, and they don't have to sue (and try to collect from) the grantor.

Taking Care of Encumbrances

Most encumbrances can simply be paid off, leaving title to the property clear and free to be transferred. The most obvious example is the deed of trust. When you want to transfer property that is subject to a trust deed, you must do one of three things: pay it off, get the buyer to assume the loan, or get the buyer to take the property "subject to" the deed of trust. Assumption of a loan, which means that the new owner takes responsibility for paying it off, is handled through the bank. Your loan agreement with the financial institution, however, may have a "due on sale" clause, which limits who can assume a loan secured by the property (see below). If the new owner takes the property "subject to" the loan, he acknowledges the loan (by including a statement in the deed) but doesn't formally assume it. If the note were foreclosed on, however, he would lose the property.

Even if the property is not encumbered, a lien can appear out of thin air if the new owner has an outstanding court judgment against him. When the transfer is made, the judgment lien attaches to the property. Transferring the property back won't get rid of the lien.

Other simple money encumbrances include:
- past-due property taxes (due twice each year, in November and February)
- mechanic's or materialman's liens, filed by people who work on your house. (A lien is a notice, recorded with the county recorder, that alerts everyone to the fact that there is a claim against the property.)
- unpaid special assessment district bond liens (for example, imposed by special hospital or drainage districts), and
- judgment liens (liens placed against your property to guarantee payment of a judgment against you in a lawsuit).

A more complicated encumbrance is a lawsuit that may affect title to your property. It shows up in the public records when a notice of the suit (a "lis pendens") is recorded in the county recorder's office. You can't get rid of this kind of encumbrance by simply paying it off. You must, however, deal with it somehow, either by passing it on to the new owner, negotiating a settlement with the party who has the claim against your property, or—if you absolutely can't avoid it—going to court to slug it out. A common method of settlement is to pay the other party something in exchange for a quitclaim deed in which she gives up any interest that she might own in the property.

> **EXAMPLE:** Andy and his brother Bill inherited some land from their uncle, but the uncle's will is being disputed in court by their cousin, Marsha. Depending on the outcome of the suit, Marsha may be determined to have some interest in the land. Andy wants to sell his half-interest to Bill, but title to the property is encumbered by a notice of the lawsuit (a "lis pendens"), which has been recorded with the county recorder. For payment of a few thousand dollars, Marsha agrees to drop the lawsuit and sign a quitclaim deed giving up all rights to the property. With the encumbrance removed, Bill can take clear title to the property.

Due on Sale Clauses

Many loan agreements contain a "due on sale" or "due on transfer" clause that makes the whole loan amount due immediately if the property is sold. And even if the existing loan can be assumed by the new owners, the terms of the loan probably require the new owners to get approval from the lender.

If a lender's approval is necessary, whether or not you will get it will probably have a lot to do with market interest rates. If interest rates have come down since the trust deed was signed, the lender will be happy to have a buyer (who has good credit) take over the loan at the relatively high interest rate. On the other hand, if rates have gone up, it will probably insist on a new loan at a higher rate of interest. If the original loan is a variable-rate loan, the lender has little incentive to be finicky unless market rates have exceeded even the maximum allowed by terms of the variable-rate loan. For this reason, variable-rate loans are often assumable.

Many people who own real property subject to a trust deed simply go ahead and transfer it, figuring the lender (who, after all, may be a large corporation at the other end of the country that bought the trust deed from a local bank), won't find out. They are often right.

Lenders do, however, have several ways to discover that the property was transferred, even if you don't tell them. A change in the name of the person making loan payments or named as beneficiary on the insurance policy often alerts a bank. Sometimes they simply call and ask for the original borrower; if the new owner says she doesn't live there, the game is up. The lender can also check (or pay someone to check) county records to see if title to the property has changed hands.

How diligent the bank is largely depends, again, on interest rates. Unless rates have gone up significantly (2% is a good general rule) since a fixed-rate loan was made, it isn't worth it to check title records all over the country to see if property has been sold. When interest rates shoot up quickly, however, and an investor holds a lot of fixed-rate loans, you can bet it is looking for transfers that will allow it to call those loans. The financial institution's policy also plays a part; some regularly use a title company to keep an eye on transfers.

Some people, to avoid notifying a bank of a transfer, don't record the deed in the county recorder's office. This is a bad idea, for all the reasons explained in Chapter 6. Experienced real estate lawyers can sometimes manage ways to get around due on sale clauses and still effectively transfer property. If a due on sale clause is a serious problem for you, talk to a lawyer.

Transfers to a living trust: If you take title to real estate in the name of a revocable living trust, your lender is forbidden by federal law from invoking a due on sale clause. (Garn-St. Germain Depository Institutions Act of 1982, 96 Stat. 1505.)

Property Tax Reassessment

Many real estate transfers trigger a reassessment of the property for local property tax purposes. Reassessment usually means a higher assessed value and a higher property tax bill. (If it's not transferred, property is usually reassessed once a year according to a standard formula that allows an increase of up to 2% in the assessed value of the property.)

State law exempts some kinds of transfers from the reassessment requirement. If, under state law, a transfer is not considered a "change of ownership," the property is not subject to reassessment. (Rev. & Tax. Code §§ 62, 63.) Many intrafamily transfers of the type discussed in this book do not trigger reassessment, including:

- A transfer between spouses or registered domestic partners, or one that takes effect at the death of one spouse or partner or at dissolution of the marriage.

  EXAMPLE: When Allen marries Maureen, he wants to add her name to the title of his house, so he signs a deed from himself to both of them. The house will not be reassessed.

- Correction of a deed.

  EXAMPLE: When Denise makes out a deed to Paula, she mistakenly types "Paul" instead. To correct this mistake, which could cause confusion later on, she makes a new deed with the correct name.

- A transfer to a revocable living trust, or by the trustee back to the person who set up the trust.

  EXAMPLE: Don wants to put some property in a living trust for his children so they will inherit it outside probate when he dies. He signs a grant deed to formally transfer the property to himself as trustee of the trust.

- Any transfer between co-owners that changes only the method of holding title, without changing the proportional interests of the co-owners.

  EXAMPLE: Ray and his cousin Lee inherited property together and take title to it in joint tenancy, which carries with it an automatic right of survivorship. They want to change the way title is held to a tenancy in common so that each can leave his share to his spouse. To do this, they execute a deed from themselves as joint tenants to themselves as tenants in common. No reassessment will be made.

- Creation of a joint tenancy *if* one of the original owners is one of the new joint tenants.

  EXAMPLE: Martha wants to put title to her house in joint tenancy with her daughter. She executes a deed from herself to her daughter and herself as joint tenants.

- Execution of a deed of trust.

  EXAMPLE: Frank wants to borrow money from his parents, using his house as security for the loan. Frank signs a deed of trust, giving a trustee the power to sell the house and pay off the loan to his parents if he defaults.

- Transfer between former spouses or registered domestic partners in connection with a property settlement agreement or decree of dissolution of marriage or partnership.

  EXAMPLE: Luke and Lisa are divorced. The property settlement agreement states that Lisa will transfer her interest in the couple's house to Luke.

- Transfer of the transferor's principal residence (and up to $1 million of other real property), in a transfer between parents and their children.

    EXAMPLE: Sarah and Ben want to transfer title to some land they own to their children. As long as their equity in the land is less than $1 million, they can transfer it without triggering a reassessment.

If you fall into one of these exempt categories, you may have to sign a form provided by the assessor. If your property will be reassessed, the county assessor will send you (after you record your deed) a Change of Ownership Statement. Instructions for filling it out are in Chapter 6.

Gifts of Real Property: Federal Gift Tax

If a gift of real property is large enough, the giver may have to file a federal gift tax return. But even if you are required to file a return, you probably won't ever have to pay tax, because a large amount of property is exempt from tax. (See Section 3, below.)

You don't have to worry about gift tax if the property:

- is being sold for its approximate fair market value (the amount your house could fetch if sold on the open market) or
- is being given away, but the value of the equity (the total value of the property minus the amount owed on it) being given is less than $12,000 per recipient ($24,000 if a married couple is giving it), or
- is being given by one spouse to the other and the recipient spouse is a U.S. citizen.

What If You're Not Sure Your Transfer Is Exempt?

You may want to file a gift tax return even if you think your transaction is exempt from tax. Filing a return can give you some peace of mind if you worry that the IRS might someday challenge your claim to exemption.

For example, say you think the property you're giving your son has a fair market value of $10,000 and is thus exempt from gift tax. How do you know that the IRS, years later, won't decide that the fair market value was $17,000 and that you should have filed a gift tax return? After all, fair market value is sometimes an inexact concept.

If you file a gift tax return announcing that the transaction is exempt, the IRS has three years to challenge it. If you don't file a return, it could still contest the tax status of the transfer years later, when you die and your final gift/estate tax is calculated.

This is a book on transfers, not taxes, and doesn't cover the subject of gift tax in detail. What we can do is alert you to potential problems and outline strategies you may want to pursue. With that warning, here are the basics of federal gift tax law.

Overview of the Federal Gift and Estate Tax

The federal gift/estate tax strikes when a property owner gives away property or leaves it at death. Most people never owe any gift/estate tax, because you can give away or leave a large amount of property tax-free. California does not levy inheritance or gift tax.

True to its name, the tax is levied on gifts and estates alike. By taxing property that's given before death, the gift tax thwarts people who try to avoid the estate tax by giving their property away before they die.

Many gifts, however, are always exempt from gift taxation, as discussed below.

What Is a Gift?

Sometimes you may not be positive whether or not the transfer you are making is in fact a gift. A gift, in the eyes of the law, is any voluntary transfer of property made without receiving anything (or receiving less than its value) in exchange. For example, if you transfer property that you know is worth $50,000 to your son and take $10,000 in exchange, you have made a gift of $40,000.

Generally, a transfer is not a gift unless you intend it to be. But the IRS doesn't know, when you transfer something for less than its market value, whether you intend to make a gift or you're just a poor businessperson. So it does the only thing it can do—it looks at the objective evidence and demands gift taxes only if a transaction doesn't appear reasonable from an economic point of view. Don't expect the IRS to accept your simple statement that, despite every indication to the contrary, your transfer of a house to your son for $1 is just a bargain, not a gift. You will be held to have intended a gift when you know at the time that you are taking less than the fair market value for the property.

How the Gift and Estate Tax Works

The gift and estate tax is a concern for only the wealthiest citizens. The amount you can leave without paying tax is scheduled to increase until the estate tax goes away entirely in 2010, though Congress may revisit the law before then.

After that, the gift tax will survive, but everyone will get a $1 million exemption. So unless you plan to make at least $1 million in taxable gifts (and most ordinary gifts are not taxable), gift tax will not be worth a second thought.

The Future of the Gift and Estate Tax		
Year	**Estate tax exemption**	**Gift tax exemption**
2007-08	$2 million	$1 million
2009	$3.5 million	$1 million
2010	Estate tax repealed	$1 million (gift tax only)
2011	$1 million (Estate tax returns unless Congress extends the repeal)	$1 million

If you make nonexempt gifts, you have to file a gift tax return with your regular income tax return. But your liability for estate and gift tax cannot be figured until you have either died or given away more than the total exempt amount in nonexempt gifts. (Exemptions are explained below.) Every time you make a nonexempt gift, you use up some of your gift tax exemption.

EXAMPLE: During his lifetime, Frank makes nonexempt gifts that total $28,000. That uses up $28,000 of his gift tax exemption; the rest of the exemption is available for property he leaves at his death.

What Gifts Are Taxable

Any gift worth more than $12,000 given to one person in one year is subject to the federal gift tax. (The giver, not the recipient, is taxed.) Each member of a married couple gets the $12,000 exclusion, so together they can give up to $24,000 per recipient tax-free. (The amount is indexed for inflation and may rise in the future.)

EXAMPLE 1: Joe gives real estate in which he has equity of $10,000 to each of his three children. He need not file a gift tax return.

EXAMPLE 2: Robin gives her son Ralph $6,000 in cash and $10,000 in real estate in one calendar year. Because the total is over the $12,000 limit, she must file a gift tax return. She will not have to pay tax now but will use part of her tax credit. Had Robin waited until January 1 of the next year to give the real estate, both gifts would have been entirely exempt.

EXAMPLE 3: In one year, Anne and her husband Peter give real estate worth $120,000 and subject to a deed of trust for $80,000 to their daughter Sophie and her husband Jeff. The total value of the gift is thus $40,000. Anne and Peter do not need to file a gift tax return. Anne and Peter each can give $12,000 per recipient, and there are two recipients, so up to $48,000 is exempt.

Some types of gifts are always exempt: gifts made to one's spouse (if the spouse is a U.S. citizen) or to tax-exempt organizations are always tax-free, no matter what the amount. So are gifts made directly for medical bills or school tuition. Gifts to a noncitizen spouse are tax-exempt up to $120,000 per year.

EXAMPLE: Francine owns a large undeveloped tract of land that is home to a diverse group of animals and plants, some of them rare. To preserve its wild state, she gives the land to the Nature Conservancy, a tax-exempt organization that acquires land to help preserve native animal and plant life. Her equity in the property is $800,000. The gift is exempt from gift tax, so it doesn't affect the amount she can leave at death tax-free.

 Not surprisingly, people have figured out some clever ways to reduce or avoid their gift and estate tax liability. If you want to delve into the subject of gift-giving as an estate planning device, see *Plan Your Estate*, by Denis Clifford and Cora Jordan (Nolo).

Disclosure Requirements

State or local law may require you to make several kinds of written disclosures about the property to the new owners before the transfer goes through.

Real Estate Transfer Disclosure Statement

If you're selling residential (not commercial) real property, you will probably have to disclose to the buyer certain information about the property's condition. (Civ. Code § 1102.) The disclosure covers all major structures and systems on the property. For example, you must tell the buyer of significant defects in the driveway, electrical system, plumbing, roof, and foundation. A buyer then has three days to back out of the sale.

You must fill out the disclosure form shown below unless:
- the transfer is a gift
- the transfer is to a co-owner, spouse, former spouse, or direct descendant or ancestor (uncles and aunts, brothers and sisters, and cousins are not exempt, since they are not direct descendants), or
- the transfer is from a trustee, guardian, or conservator.

A tear-out copy is included in the appendix. The form is changed by the legislature fairly regularly; be sure you use the most recent version. If it has changed since this book was published, you can get a copy from a real estate broker or title company, or from the law library—look up California Civil Code Section 1102.6. To find this statute online, go to Nolo's website at www.nolo.com and follow the links to the California statutes.

The completed form must be personally delivered or mailed to the buyer before title is transferred. The buyer has three days after the form is delivered (five days after the date of mailing, if the form is mailed) to give the seller a written withdrawal of the offer to purchase the property. (Civ. Code § 1102.2.)

The seller doesn't have to hire professionals to answer the questions on the disclosure form. The seller must, however, fill out the form in good faith

Real Estate Transfer Disclosure Statement

(CALIFORNIA CIVIL CODE § 1102, ET SEQ.)

THIS DISCLOSURE STATEMENT CONCERNS THE REAL PROPERTY SITUATED IN THE CITY OF _____ ,

COUNTY OF _____ , STATE OF CALIFORNIA, DESCRIBED AS _____

_____ .

THIS STATEMENT IS A DISCLOSURE OF THE CONDITION OF THE ABOVE-DESCRIBED PROPERTY IN COMPLIANCE

WITH SECTION 1102 OF THE CIVIL CODE AS OF _____ , _____ . IT IS NOT A WARRANTY

OF ANY KIND BY THE SELLER(S) OR ANY AGENT(S) REPRESENTING ANY PRINCIPAL(S) IN THIS TRANSACTION, AND IT

IS NOT A SUBSTITUTE FOR ANY INSPECTIONS OR WARRANTIES THE PRINCIPAL(S) MAY WISH TO OBTAIN.

I

COORDINATION WITH OTHER DISCLOSURE FORMS

This Real Estate Transfer Disclosure Statement is made pursuant to Section 1102 of the Civil Code. Other statutes require disclosures, depending upon the details of the particular real estate transaction (for example: special study zone and purchase-money liens on residential property).

Substituted Disclosures: The following disclosures and other disclosures required by law, including the Natural Hazard Disclosure Report/Statement that may include airport annoyances, earthquake, fire, flood, or special assessment information, have or will be made in connection with this real estate transfer, and are intended to satisfy the disclosure obligations on this form, where the subject matter is the same:

☐ Inspection reports completed pursuant to the contract of sale or receipt for deposit.

☐ Additional inspection reports or disclosures:

_____

_____

_____ .

(List all substituted disclosure forms to be used in connection with this transaction.)

II

SELLER'S INFORMATION

The Seller discloses the following information with the knowledge that even though this is not a warranty, prospective Buyers may rely on this information in deciding whether and on what terms to purchase the subject property. Seller hereby authorizes any agent(s) representing any principal(s) in this transaction to provide a copy of this statement to any person or entity in connection with any actual or anticipated sale of the property.

THE FOLLOWING ARE REPRESENTATIONS MADE BY THE SELLER(S) AND ARE NOT THE REPRESENTATIONS OF THE AGENT(S), IF ANY. THIS INFORMATION IS A DISCLOSURE AND IT IS NOT INTENDED TO BE PART OF ANY CONTRACT BETWEEN THE BUYER AND SELLER.

Seller ☐ is ☐ is not occupying the property.

A. The subject property has the items checked below (read across):

☐ Range	☐ Oven	☐ Microwave
☐ Dishwasher	☐ Trash Compactor	☐ Garbage Disposal
☐ Washer/Dryer Hookups	☐ Rain Gutters	☐ Smoke Detector(s)
☐ Fire Alarm	☐ T.V. Antenna	☐ Satellite Dish
☐ Intercom	☐ Central Heating	☐ Central Air Conditioning
☐ Evaporator Cooler(s)	☐ Wall/Window Air Conditioning	☐ Sprinklers

Real Estate Transfer Disclosure Statement, continued

☐ Public Sewer System   ☐ Septic Tank   ☐ Sump Pump

☐ Water Softener   ☐ Patio/Decking   ☐ Built-in Barbecue

☐ Sauna   ☐ Gazebo   ☐ Burglar Alarms

☐ Hot Tub ☐ Locking Safety Cover* ☐ Pool ☐ Child Resistant Barrier* ☐ Spa ☐ Locking Safety Cover*

☐ Security Gate(s)   ☐ Automatic Garage Door Opener(s)* ☐ # of Remote Controls _____

☐ Garage: ☐ Attached ☐ Not Attached ☐ Carport

☐ Pool/Spa Heater: ☐ Gas   ☐ Solar   ☐ Electric

☐ Water Heater: ☐ Gas   ☐ Water Heater Anchored, Braced, or Strapped*   ☐ Electric

☐ Water Supply: ☐ City   ☐ Well   ☐ Private Utility
                    ☐ Other _____

☐ Gas Supply: ☐ Utility   ☐ Bottled

☐ Window Screens   ☐ Window Security Bars ☐ Quick Release Mechanism on Bedroom Windows*

☐ Exhaust Fan(s) in _____   ☐ 220 Volt Wiring in _____

☐ Fireplace(s) in _____   ☐ Gas Starter _____

☐ Roof(s): Type: _____   ☐ Age: _____ (approx.)

☐ Other: _____

Are there, to the best of your (Seller's) knowledge, any of the above that are not in operating condition?

☐ Yes   ☐ No   If yes, then describe. (Attach additional sheets if necessary.)

_____

_____

_____

_____

B. Are you (Seller) aware of any significant defects/malfunctions in any of the following?

☐ Yes   ☐ No   If yes, check appropriate box(es) below.

☐ Interior Walls   ☐ Ceilings   ☐ Floors   ☐ Exterior Walls   ☐ Insulation

☐ Roof(s)   ☐ Windows   ☐ Doors   ☐ Foundation   ☐ Slab(s)

☐ Driveways   ☐ Sidewalks   ☐ Walls/Fences   ☐ Electrical Systems   ☐ Plumbing/Sewers/Septics

☐ Other Structural Components (describe):

_____

_____

_____

If any of the above is checked, explain. (Attach additional sheets if necessary.) _____

_____

_____

_____

*This garage door opener or child resistant pool barrier may not be in compliance with the safety standards relating to automatic reversing devices as set forth in Chapter 12.5 (commencing with Section 19890) of Part 3 of Division 13, or with the pool safety standards of Article 2.5 (commencing with Section 115920) of Chapter 5 of Part 10 of Division 104, of the Health and Safety Code. The water heater may not be anchored, braced, or strapped in accordance with Section 19211 of the Health and Safety Code. Window security bars may not have quick release mechanisms in compliance with the 1995 Edition of the California Building Standards Code.

Real Estate Transfer Disclosure Statement, continued

C. Are you (Seller) aware of any of the following:

1. Substances, materials, or products that may be an environmental hazard such as, but not limited to, asbestos, formaldehyde, radon gas, lead-based paint, mold, fuel or chemical storage tanks, and contaminated soil or water on the subject property. ☐ Yes ☐ No

2. Features of the property shared in common with adjoining landowners, such as walls, fences, and driveways, whose use or responsibility for maintenance may have an effect on the subject property. ☐ Yes ☐ No

3. Any encroachments, easements, or similar matters that may affect your interest in the subject property. ☐ Yes ☐ No

4. Room additions, structural modifications, or other alterations or repairs made without necessary permits. ☐ Yes ☐ No

5. Room additions, structural modifications, or other alterations or repairs not in compliance with building codes. ☐ Yes ☐ No

6. Fill (compacted or otherwise) on the property or any portion thereof. ☐ Yes ☐ No

7. Any settling from any cause, or slippage, sliding, or other soil problems. ☐ Yes ☐ No

8. Flooding, drainage, or grading problems. ☐ Yes ☐ No

9. Major damage to the property or any other structures from fire, earthquake, floods, or landslides. ☐ Yes ☐ No

10. Any zoning violations, nonconforming uses, or violations of "setback" requirements. ☐ Yes ☐ No

11. Neighborhood noise problems or other nuisances. ☐ Yes ☐ No

12. CC&Rs or other deed restrictions or obligations. ☐ Yes ☐ No

13. Homeowners' association that has any authority over the subject property. ☐ Yes ☐ No

14. Any "common area" (facilities such as pools, tennis courts, walkways, or other areas co-owned in undivided interest with others). ☐ Yes ☐ No

15. Any notices of abatement or citations against the property. ☐ Yes ☐ No

16. Any lawsuits by or against the Seller threatening to or affecting this real property, including any lawsuits alleging a defect or deficiency in this real property or "common areas" (facilities such as pools, tennis courts, walkways, or other areas co-owned in undivided interest with others). ☐ Yes ☐ No

If the answer to any of these is yes, explain (attach additional sheets if necessary): _____

_____

Seller certifies that the information herein is true and correct to the best of the Seller's knowledge as of the date signed by the Seller.

Seller _____   Date _____

Seller _____   Date _____

Real Estate Transfer Disclosure Statement, continued

III

AGENT'S INSPECTION DISCLOSURE (LISTING AGENT)

(To be completed only if the Seller is represented by an agent in this transaction.)

THE UNDERSIGNED, BASED ON THE ABOVE INQUIRY OF THE SELLER(S) AS TO THE CONDITION OF THE PROPERTY AND BASED ON REASONABLY COMPETENT AND DILIGENT VISUAL INSPECTION OF THE ACCESSIBLE AREAS OF THE PROPERTY IN CONJUNCTION WITH THAT INQUIRY, STATES THE FOLLOWING:

☐ Agent notes no items for disclosure.

☐ Agent notes the following items: _____

Agent (Print Name of Broker Representing Seller): _____

By (Associate Licensee or Broker's Signature) _____

Date _____

IV

AGENT'S INSPECTION DISCLOSURE (SELLING AGENT)

(To be completed only if the agent who has obtained the offer is other than the agent above.)

THE UNDERSIGNED, BASED ON A REASONABLY COMPETENT AND DILIGENT VISUAL INSPECTION OF THE ACCESSIBLE AREAS OF THE PROPERTY, STATES THE FOLLOWING:

☐ Agent notes no items for disclosure.

☐ Agent notes the following items: _____

Agent (Print Name of Broker Obtaining Offer) _____

By (Associate Licensee or Broker's Signature) _____

Date _____

V

BUYER(S) AND SELLER(S) MAY WISH TO OBTAIN PROFESSIONAL ADVICE AND/OR INSPECTIONS OF THE PROPERTY AND TO PROVIDE FOR APPROPRIATE PROVISIONS IN A CONTRACT BETWEEN BUYER(S) AND SELLER(S) WITH RESPECT TO ANY ADVICE/INSPECTION/DEFECTS.

I/WE ACKNOWLEDGE RECEIPT OF A COPY OF THIS STATEMENT.

Seller _____   Date _____

Seller _____   Date _____

Buyer _____   Date _____

Buyer _____   Date _____

Agent (Print Name of Broker Representing Seller) _____

By (Associate Licensee or Broker's Signature) _____

Date _____

Agent (Print Name of Broker Obtaining the Offer) _____

By (Associate Licensee or Broker's Signature) _____

Date _____

SECTION 1102.3 OF THE CIVIL CODE PROVIDES A BUYER WITH THE RIGHT TO RESCIND A PURCHASE CONTRACT FOR AT LEAST THREE DAYS AFTER THE DELIVERY OF THIS DISCLOSURE IF DELIVERY OCCURS AFTER THE SIGNING OF AN OFFER TO PURCHASE. IF YOU WISH TO RESCIND THE CONTRACT, YOU MUST ACT WITHIN THE PRESCRIBED PERIOD. A REAL ESTATE BROKER IS QUALIFIED TO ADVISE ON REAL ESTATE. IF YOU DESIRE LEGAL ADVICE, CONSULT YOUR ATTORNEY.

and honestly and must take "ordinary care" in obtaining the information. This means that the seller is responsible for including information about the property that he or she knows or, as a reasonable homeowner, should know.

If you don't know and can't find out (by making a reasonable effort) some of the information requested on the form, you may make a "reasonable approximation" as long as you make it clear (on the form) that the information is an approximation that is based on the best information available to you.

If an error or omission is carelessly or intentionally made in the statement, the sale is still valid, but the seller is liable for any actual damages the buyer suffers. For example, if you sell your house and forget to disclose the fact that the roof leaks (and you know or should know it does), the sale is still good, but if the buyer sues you, you'll have to pay for the damage that the leak causes and the cost of repairs.

You should take seriously your responsibility to disclose problems and err on the side of more, rather than less, disclosure. Many homeowners, although it is not required by the law, are choosing to protect themselves by hiring (or encouraging the buyer to hire) a general contractor to inspect the house and write a report on its condition. Home-inspection firms are popping up in response to the demand. An inspection and written report for an average-sized house costs from about $250 to $550. If you do get a report, make sure the new owner gets a copy and acknowledges its receipt in writing.

Natural Hazard Disclosure Statement

The Real Estate Transfer Disclosure Statement includes information on many hazards affecting the house, some of which require additional disclosures. State law requires sellers to provide buyers with a Natural Hazard Disclosure Statement indicating if the property is in one of six hazard zones (Civ. Code § 1102.6c):

- a flood hazard zone designated by the Federal Emergency Management Agency (FEMA) (42 U.S.C. §§ 4001 and following)

- an area of potential flooding due to failure of a dam as identified by the Office of Emergency Services on an "inundation map" (Gov't. Code § 8589.5.)
- a very high fire hazard severity zone designated by a local agency (Gov't. Code §§ 51178, 51179, 51182, 51183.5)
- a state-designated wildland fire area zone (Pub. Res. Code §§ 4125, 4136)
- a delineated earthquake fault zone as identified by the California State Geologist (Pub. Res. Code §§ 2621.9, 2622), or
- a seismic hazards zone (area where landslides and liquefaction are most likely to occur) as defined under Pub. Res. Code §§ 2694, 2696.

These designations are often puzzling, at least to a layperson. For example, San Francisco is not within an earthquake fault zone. That's because the fault line isn't in San Francisco—although San Francisco has certainly experienced the ravages of earthquakes. Also, sometimes the available maps and information are not of sufficient accuracy or scale for a seller to determine whether or not his property falls inside or outside of a designated hazard zone, such as a high fire hazard severity zone. In this case, the law requires the seller to mark "Yes" on the Natural Hazard Disclosure Statement—unless the seller has evidence, such as a report from a licensed engineer, that the property is not in the fire hazard zone. (Civ. Code § 1102.4.)

A blank Natural Hazard Disclosure Statement (NHDS) is included in the appendix.

Earthquake and Seismic Disclosures

In addition to the Natural Hazard Disclosure Statement, state law requires sellers to provide information on the safety of the house itself and its ability to resist earthquakes.

Residential Earthquake Hazards Report

The seller must disclose any known seismic deficiencies on the property, such as whether or not the house is bolted or anchored to the foundation and whether cripple walls, if any, are braced. (Gov't.

Natural Hazard Disclosure Statement

This statement applies to the following property: _____

The transferor and his or her agent(s) or a third-party consultant disclose the following information with the knowledge that even though this is not a warranty, prospective transferees may rely on this information in deciding whether and on what terms to purchase the subject property. Transferor hereby authorizes any agent(s) representing any principal(s) in this action to provide a copy of this statement to any person or entity in connection with any actual or anticipated sale of the property.

The following are representations made by the transferor and his or her agent(s) based on their knowledge and maps drawn by the state and federal governments. This information is a disclosure and is not intended to be part of any contract between the transferee and transferor.

THIS REAL PROPERTY LIES WITHIN THE FOLLOWING HAZARDOUS AREA(S):

A SPECIAL FLOOD HAZARD AREA (Any type Zone "A" or "V") designated by the Federal Emergency Management Agency.

☐ Yes   ☐ No   ☐ Do not know and information not available from local jurisdiction

AN AREA OF POTENTIAL FLOODING shown on a dam failure inundation map pursuant to Section 8589.5 of the Government Code.

☐ Yes   ☐ No   ☐ Do not know and information not available from local jurisdiction

A VERY HIGH FIRE HAZARD SEVERITY ZONE pursuant to Section 51178 or 51179 of the Government Code. The owner of this property is subject to the maintenance requirements of Section 51182 of the Government Code.

☐ Yes   ☐ No

A WILDLAND AREA THAT MAY CONTAIN SUBSTANTIAL FOREST FIRE RISKS AND HAZARDS pursuant to Section 4125 of the Public Resources Code. The owner of this property is subject to the maintenance requirements of Section 4291 of the Public Resources Code. Additionally, it is not the state's responsibility to provide fire protection services to any building or structure located within the wildlands unless the Department of Forestry and Fire Protection has entered into a cooperative agreement with a local agency for those purposes pursuant to Section 4142 of the Public Resources Code.

☐ Yes   ☐ No

AN EARTHQUAKE FAULT ZONE pursuant to Section 2622 of the Public Resources Code.

☐ Yes   ☐ No

A SEISMIC HAZARD ZONE pursuant to Section 2696 of the Public Resources Code.

Landslide Zone   ☐ Yes   ☐ No   ☐ Map not yet released by state
Liquefaction Zone   ☐ Yes   ☐ No   ☐ Map not yet released by state

THESE HAZARDS MAY LIMIT YOUR ABILITY TO DEVELOP THE REAL PROPERTY, TO OBTAIN INSURANCE, OR TO RECEIVE ASSISTANCE AFTER A DISASTER.

THE MAPS ON WHICH THESE DISCLOSURES ARE BASED ESTIMATE WHERE NATURAL HAZARDS EXIST. THEY ARE NOT DEFINITIVE INDICATORS OF WHETHER OR NOT A PROPERTY WILL BE AFFECTED BY A NATURAL DISASTER. BUYER(S) AND SELLER(S) MAY WISH TO OBTAIN PROFESSIONAL ADVICE REGARDING THOSE HAZARDS AND OTHER HAZARDS THAT MAY AFFECT THE PROPERTY.

Signature of Transferor(s):_____ Date: _____

Code § 8897.) The seller is not required to hire anyone to evaluate the house or to strengthen any weaknesses that exist. If the house was built in 1960 or later, oral disclosure is enough.

If the house was built before 1960, the seller must disclose in writing and sign the disclosure form, Residential Earthquake Hazards Report, included in a booklet called the *Homeowner's Guide to Earthquake Safety*. The seller must give the buyer a copy of this booklet and disclosure "as soon as practicable before the transfer." The *Homeowner's Guide to Earthquake Safety* is available from the Seismic Safety Commission (SSC), 1755 Creekside Oaks Drive, Suite 100, Sacramento, CA 95833. You can phone the SSC at 916-263-5506 or check its website at www.seismic.ca.gov.

Water Heater Bracing

All water heaters must be braced, anchored, or strapped to resist falling or displacement during an earthquake. (Health and Safety Code § 19211.) Anyone selling property with such a water heater must certify in writing (on the Real Estate Transfer Disclosure Statement) that the heater complies with the law.

Environmental Hazards

Item C.1 on the Real Estate Transfer Disclosure Statement asks the seller to identify environmental hazards on the property, such as radon gas and contaminated soil. In addition, sellers should provide prospective homebuyers a copy of *Environmental Hazards: A Guide for Homeowners and Buyers,* which provides information on different environmental hazards which may be on or near the property, such as asbestos, formaldehyde, lead, and hazardous wastes, and lists federal and state agencies and publications for more information. This booklet is published by the California Department of Real Estate, the California Environmental Protection Agency, and the Department of Health Services, and is available from the California Association of Realtors (CAR). For price and order information, call CAR at its Los Angeles office at 213-739-8200 or check out its website at www.car.org.

Lead

HUD rules require that applicants for FHA mortgages be given a lead-based paint notice disclosure form before signing the final sales contract. Lead paint in homes financed by the FHA must be removed or repainted.

California law requires that a seller disclose lead-based paint hazards to prospective buyers on the Real Estate Transfer Disclosure Statement. (Civ. Code § 1102.6.) Furthermore, sellers of houses built before 1978 must comply with the Residential Lead-Based Paint Hazard Reduction Act of 1992 (42 U.S.C. § 2852d), also known as Title X. Sellers must:

- attach a federally required disclosure form, "Disclosure of Information on Lead-Based Paint and/or Lead-Based Paint Hazards," to every sales contract for residences built prior to 1978, and disclose any known lead hazards in the house or outbuildings
- give buyers a pamphlet prepared by the U.S. Environmental Protection Agency (EPA) called *Protect Your Family from Lead in Your Home*
- keep signed acknowledgments for three years as proof of compliance, and
- give buyers a ten-day opportunity to test the housing for lead.

If a seller fails to comply with Title X requirements, a buyer can sue the seller for triple the amount of damages.

Resources on Lead

The National Lead Information Clearinghouse has extensive information on lead hazards, prevention, and disclosures. For more information, call the Clearinghouse at 800-424-LEAD or check its website at www.epa.gov/lead. You can find an online version of the required disclosure pamphlet *Protect Your Family from Lead in Your Home* by choosing the form and the "Brochures and Training" link on the EPA site.

Natural Hazard Disclosure Statement, continued

Agent represents that the information herein is true and correct to the best of the agent's knowledge as of the date signed by the agent.

Signature of Agent(s):_____ Date: _____

Signature of Agent(s):_____ Date: _____

Check only one of the following:

☐ Transferor(s) and their agent(s) represent that the information herein is true and correct to the best of their knowledge as of the date signed by the transferor(s) and agent(s).

☐ Transferor(s) and their agent(s) acknowledge that they have exercised good faith in the selection of a third-party report provider as required in Civil Code Section 1103.7, and that the representations made in this Natural Hazard Disclosure Statement are based upon information provided by the independent third-party disclosure provider as a substituted disclosure pursuant to Civil Code Section 1103.4. Neither transferor(s) nor their agent(s) (1) has independently verified the information contained in this statement and report or (2) is personally aware of any errors or inaccuracies in the information contained on the statement. This statement was prepared by the provider below:

Third-Party Disclosure Provider(s) _____ Date _____

Transferee represents that he or she has read and understands this document.

Pursuant to Civil Code Section 1103.8, the representations made in this Natural Hazard Disclosure Statement do not constitute all of the transferor's or agent's disclosure obligations in this transaction.

Signature of Transferee(s) _____ Date _____

Signature of Transferee(s)_____ Date _____

Disclosure of Deaths

State law implies that the seller should disclose any deaths known to have occurred on the property within the past three years. If a death occurred more than three years ago, the seller need disclose it only if asked. (*Reed v. King,* 145 Cal.App.3d 261 (1983).)

Military Ordnance

Sellers who know of any former federal or state ordnance locations (once used for military training purposes which may contain potentially explosive munitions) within one mile of the property must provide written disclosure to the buyer as soon as practicable before transfer of title. (Civ. Code § 1102.15.)

Registered Sex Offenders (Megan's Law)

Contracts for the sale of a house or other residential property must include a notice, in not less than eight-point type, regarding the availability of a database maintained by law enforcement authorities on the location of registered sex offenders. (Civ. Code § 2079.10a.) This database is available through a "900" telephone service. Callers must have specific information about individuals they are checking, and information regarding neighborhoods is not available.

The seller or broker is not required to provide additional information about the proximity of registered sex offenders. The law clearly states, however, that it does not change the existing responsibilities of sellers and real estate brokers to make disclosures of "material facts" that would affect the "value and desirability" of a property. This means that a seller or broker who knew for a fact that a registered sex offender lived next door or a few houses down would be responsible for disclosing this "material" fact to the buyer.

For more information on this disclosure require-ment, check out http://caag.state.ca.us.megan. A contract containing the necessary language is in *For Sale by Owner in California,* by George Devine (Nolo).

Local Disclosure Requirements

Many cities and counties have local disclosure requirements and you may be required to use an additional form. For example, in Los Angeles, sellers must disclose applicable zoning laws. Check with the city or county planning or building department to find out about any local requirements. You may need a special form, the Local Option Real Estate Transfer Disclosure Statement. (Civ. Code § 1102.6a.) A blank form is included in the appendix.

Documentary Transfer Tax

You don't have to worry about this tax if the transfer is a gift.

This tax, which is based on the sale price of the property, is collected by the county recorder when a deed is recorded. No documentary transfer tax is due unless the property is sold. For example, a gift (including a transfer to a revocable living trust) or a transfer pursuant to a court order is exempt from the tax.

The basic tax rate is 55¢ per $500 of the sales price. Some cities add surtaxes so that the total rate is considerably higher. You can find out the rate in your city by calling the county recorder's office.

Transfers Before Bankruptcy

If you think you may have to declare bankruptcy, special rules may restrict your right to transfer or mortgage valuable property. If you give property away (put it in someone else's name) to frustrate the bankruptcy laws, the transfer may be considered fraudulent. (Uniform Fraudulent Transfer Act, Civ. Code §§ 3439 and following.) In some circumstances, the transfer can be voided by a court and the property used to pay your creditors. In general, transfers immediately before bankruptcy are suspect, and transfers made up to a year before bankruptcy can be trouble.

More information about property and bankruptcy. See *How to File for Chapter 7 Bankruptcy*, by Stephen Elias, Albin Renauer, and Robin Leonard and *How to File for Chapter 13 Bankruptcy*, by Stephen Elias and Robin Leonard, both published by Nolo.

Do You Need a Title Search and Title Insurance?

As discussed briefly above, title insurance is a way for a buyer (or lender financing a purchase) to be sure that if there's a problem with the title to the property he's just bought, the title insurance company will make it good. Insurance protects the buyer against problems that have already occurred. For example, suppose somebody once put the wrong property description on a deed, forged an owner's signature, forgot to get her spouse to sign the deed, or otherwise messed up. If for some reason a title search doesn't disclose the error, insurance will protect the buyer and lender. Title insurance doesn't protect against acts of the government such as condemnation proceedings or zoning restrictions.

Family Forgery

Title insurance also protects buyers from the consequences of forged deeds. You may not think you need to check the title records of your property for forged documents, but forgeries by family members are on the rise, according to title insurance companies. A common scenario is forgery by a son or daughter who forges parents' names on a deed of trust making the property security for a loan. The child figures the parents may never find out about it if the loan is paid off and the child inherits the property anyway.

Title Searches

A title search turns up encumbrances on the title to property. If you don't know what encumbrances may exist on the property you want to transfer, and having this information is important (for example, the property is going to new owners, or a significant sum is being paid for the transfer), you will definitely want to have a title search. If, on the other hand, you know no encumbrances exist or your transfer involves a change of title (for example, from tenancy in common to joint tenancy) but no new owners, you probably won't need a title search (though it never hurts).

A title search gives you an accurate picture of who owns the property and turns up most kinds of claims others may have against it. Specifically, a title search tells you if:

- the property has been pledged as security for a loan
- an easement has been granted
- certain liens (claims that prevent title to the property from being transferred until the lienholder (creditor) is paid the lien amount) have been placed on the property
- the property taxes haven't been paid
- a lawsuit has been filed contesting ownership of the property, or
- a prior deed (say, the one transferring the property to whomever you got it from) was invalid.

A title search should check the validity of all prior transfers of the property. This string of transfers, which in California often stretches back in time to grants from the Mexican or United States governments in the 19th century, is called the chain of title. If a deed to the land was ever improperly executed, or the property description in the deed was wrong, and the error went uncorrected, the current owner may not hold valid title to the land. Theoretically, all transfers are recorded in the public records. If evidence of a transfer—a link in the chain of title—is missing, that's a problem in itself, and it may necessitate a trip to court to resolve any uncertainty.

These days, title insurance companies may not actually check all the old transfers. They rely on previous checks and just make sure there are no new problems with the title. Computerized records have largely replaced microfiche records, and the computer data often do not include the older transfers.

Virtually no layperson does a title search; it's a tedious, time-consuming job. And without some experience, it's easy to mess up. But if you want to be sure title to the property is clear, what should you do? Let's stop a minute and look at your options.

1. Go without a title search. If you are merely changing the way title is held and not bringing in any new owners, or putting property in a revocable living trust, you may not need a title search.

Also, if the property was transferred to the current owner fairly recently, the title was checked then (as it always is in standard transfers; a bank wouldn't think of lending money to finance the purchase of property without it), and you know that no liens or other encumbrances have been filed since, you're pretty safe not bothering with another search.

2. Get a property profile that checks the current title only. Title companies, which keep copies of the public records in their offices, furnish free "property profiles" that show the current state of the title to property (that is, without checking all the prior transfers, as a full title search would).

A property profile contains photocopies of everything in the public records that affects the property now. It typically includes:

- Cover page: This lists the property address, owner, assessed value, and property tax due.
- Grant deed: A copy of the deed that transferred title to the current owner will always be included.
- Deeds of trust: All deeds of trust recorded against the property should be included. Make sure all pages of the deeds, including attachments, are there. Many property profiles only have the first page of the trust deed,

which may not contain critical "due on sale" or "acceleration" clauses. The deed will not expressly tell you whether it is the first, second, or third deed of trust recorded against the property; that is determined by the order in which they were recorded.
- Assessor's map: This shows the subdivision map filed with the county. The map shows the lots and boundaries of the property and also the assessor's parcel number (APN), which the assessor uses on the tax bills. It's critical that you check the legal description and APN given on your grant deed against what's on this map.

3. Pay a pro to do the title search. For $100 to $250 or so, you can hire a title company to conduct a title search of your property. The fee is one of those "closing costs" that every buyer of real estate has come to know and love. The company will search the public records and issue a report showing:

- the legal owner's name
- all liens, restrictions, easements, and other encumbrances
- the legal description of the property, and
- local property taxes that have been assessed.

Some title companies do not sell title reports separately; you must also buy title insurance. The price of insurance depends on the value of the property; $1,000 to $1,500 for property worth $100,000 is a good estimate. You may need to make a few phone calls to find a company in your area that will do a title search separately.

4. Do the search yourself. If you're a diehard do-it-yourselfer, and have plenty of spare time, you can try to do the search yourself, but it's not a cost-effective way to spend your time. (And a title company won't insure a title that it hasn't checked itself.)

To search the title to property you must start with the "Grantor-Grantee Index" (usually kept on microfiche) at the county recorder's office. In it you can look up the current owner's name and start going backwards in time from the current deed. Remember that you have a long, long way to go (more than 100 years, almost certainly), and that you'll need to check every name and legal description in every deed to the property. You will also need to look up the property in the county assessor's property tax records and the general county records that show bankruptcies, divorces, name changes, and judgments. Finally, you will need to go through the bankruptcy records of the federal district court.

Obviously, doing a title search yourself is a complex task that takes practice to get good (or even competent) at, and given the risks involved, it's well worth it to pay a professional. Moreover, when you go to sell (or borrow money on) the land later, no one will want to rely on an amateur's title search, so you'll probably end up paying for a title search sometime. For your peace of mind, if you want a title search, get it done right.

What a title search can't show. Obviously, a title search can't uncover unrecorded transfers. And no title search will reveal the extent to which California's community property laws affect ownership of the property. Those laws may mean, for example, that even if the house is in one spouse's (or domestic partner's) name alone it belongs to both and that both must sign the deed. We discuss this point, and how to handle it, in Chapter 2.

Similarly, an unmarried live-in lover may have property rights based on an implied contract. See Chapter 2.

Title Insurance

Usually, the point of having a title search is to enable you to buy title insurance. It works like this: The title insurance company searches the public records and issues a preliminary title report (the "prelim"), which shows all encumbrances of record. Then the company issues a title insurance policy, guaranteeing that the title is clear of encumbrances except those specified on the preliminary report.

The buyer's policy is in the amount of the purchase price of the property. Usually it is a CLTA (California Land Title Association) policy. If someone (including the seller) is lending money to the buyer, and the loan is secured by a deed of trust on the property, the lender usually buys a separate insurance policy that covers him for the amount of the loan. The lender's policy is often an ALTA (American Land Title Association) policy, which offers broader coverage than the standard CLTA policy.

What If the Title Search Turns Up Problems?

If there is a problem in the chain of title—meaning that somewhere along the line the property was imperfectly transferred—the current owners will have to correct the defect. Correction will entail either a new deed (often in the form of a quitclaim deed, discussed in Chapter 5) or going to court to have a judge resolve any uncertainty in who owns what.

For example, say that your father, the previous owner of the property you want to transfer, mistakenly left out a 50-foot strip of the property when he deeded the land to you. If this mistake is not corrected, the new owners will be getting less than they think they are.

What can be done to rectify the mistake? Your father can execute a new deed transferring his interest in the omitted property to you. If he were no longer living, you would have to go to court in the county where the property is located and get a judgment saying the property belongs to you. That process almost certainly requires a lawyer and is beyond the scope of this book.

COMPARISON SHOPPING MAY SAVE YOU MONEY
THIS TITLE INFORMATION HAS BEEN FURNISHED WITHOUT CHARGE BY
TITLE INSURANCE COMPANY

IN CONFORMANCE WITH THE RULES AND REGULATIONS ESTABLISHED BY THE
CALIFORNIA INSURANCE COMMISSIONER. WHO URGES YOU TO SHOP FOR THE
BEST SERVICE AVAILABLE AND COMPARE CHARGES AND FEES FOR TITLE
INSURANCE. ESCROW. AND OTHER SERVICES ASSOCIATED WITH THE
PURCHASE OR SALE OF A HOME.

PROPERTY PROFILE

ADDRESS: 5892 Eagle Creek Road

Richmond, California 94807

RECORD OWNER: REAL PROPERTIES, INC.

DEED Recording date: Sep.20,1984   Documentary transfer tax: $22.55

CONCURRENT TRUST DEED, IF ANY: (See attached)

LEGAL DESCRIPTION: (See attached deed copy and plat)

TAX INFORMATION:

Assessors Parcel No.	527-012-002
Assessed Value Land	$ 31,008
Assessed Value Improvements	$ 19,992
Exemption	$
Net Assessed Value	$ 51,000
Installments	$ 359.33
	$ 359.33

HORTON FOO
CUSTOMER SERVICE
REPRESENTATIVE

XXX TITLE INSURANCE CO.
203 SOUTH OREGON STREET
WALNUT CREEK CA 95672
415-933-7920

In lieu of the above, see attached copy of Assessment Roll.

XXX TITLE INSURANCE

This information is furnished as a public service. Although care has been taken in its preparation.
the company assumes no liability for its accuracy or completeness
Please note that concurrent trust deed information may not show all encumbrances of record.

CAA-298 W (Rev. 1-82)

WHEN RECORDED, PLEASE MAIL THIS
INSTRUMENT TO

DAVID MACLEAN
P.O. Box 1
Richmond, CA. 94801

84 137605

SEP 20 1984

Order No   49333
Escrow No   APN #527-012-002

RECORDED AT REQUEST OF
**TITLE COMPANY
OF CONTRA COSTA**

OFFICIAL RECORDS OF
CONTRA COSTA COUNTY

COUNTY RECORDER

FEE $ 700

SPACE ABOVE FOR RECORDER'S USE ONLY

④

SHORT FORM DEED OF TRUST AND ASSIGNMENT OF RENTS

This Deed of Trust, made this   17   day of   September, 1984   , between

     REAL PROPERTIES, INC. , a corporation

                                                    , herein called TRUSTOR,

whose address is   P.O. Box 682,   Berkeley CA 94702
                (number and street)   (city)   (zone)   (state)

     TITLE COMPANY OF CONTRA COSTA, a California corporation, herein called Trustee, and

     DAVID MACLEAN

                                                   , herein called BENEFICIARY.

Witnesseth: That Trustor IRREVOCABLY GRANTS, TRANSFERS AND ASSIGNS to TRUSTEE IN TRUST, WITH

POWER OF SALE, that property in City of Richmond, Contra Costa   County, California, described as:

     FOR LEGAL DESCRIPTION SEE EXHIBIT "A" ATTACHED HERETO

     FOR FURTHER TERMS AND CONDITIONS SEE EXHIBIT "B" ATTACHED HERETO

TOGETHER WITH the rents, issues and profits thereof, SUBJECT, HOWEVER, to the right, power and authority given to and conferred upon Beneficiary by paragraph (10) of the provisions incorporated herein by reference to collect and apply such rents, issues and profits

For the Purpose of Securing: 1 Performance of each agreement of Trustor incorporated by reference or contained herein 2 Payment of the indebtedness evidenced by one promissory note of even date herewith, and any extension or renewal thereof, in the principal sum of $ 18,129.72 executed by Trustor in favor of Beneficiary or order. 3. Payment of such further sums as the then record owner of said property hereafter may borrow from Beneficiary, when evidenced by another note (or notes) reciting it is so secured.

To Protect the Security of This Deed of Trust, Trustor Agrees: By the execution and delivery of this Deed of Trust and the Note secured hereby, that provisions (1) to (14), inclusive, (which provisions are printed on the reverse hereof) of the fictitious Deed of Trust recorded in the office of the County Recorder of each of the following counties in the State of California on July 3, 1968, in the Book and at the Page designated after the name of each County, which provisions are identical in each Deed of Trust, shall be and they are hereby incorporated herein and made an integral part hereof for all purposes as though set forth herein at length

CITY	REEL OR BOOK	IMAGE OR PAGE	COUNTY	REEL OR BOOK	IMAGE OR PAGE	COUNTY	REEL OR BOOK	IMAGE OR PAGE
Alameda	2210	970	San Francisco	B-254	678	Santa Cruz	1890	217
Marin	2223	30	San Joaquin	3221	325	San Mateo	5497	162
Monterey	563	919	Sonoma	2339	251	Santa Clara	8178	33
Napa	769	977	Stanislaus	2227	312	Contra Costa	5660	126
Sacramento	68 07-03	250	Solano	1515	107	El Dorado	1443	10

     The undersigned Trustor requests that a copy of any Notice of Default and of any Notice of Sale hereunder be mailed to him at his address hereinbefore set forth

STATE OF CALIFORNIA
COUNTY OF

On September 19,   19___
before me, the undersigned, a Notary Public in and for said County and State personally appeared   Diane A. Holst

known to me to be the   President and
James B. Holst

known to me to be the   Secretary of

**OFFICIAL SEAL
CASSY PEAR
NOTARY PUBLIC CALIFORNIA
CONTRA COSTA COUNTY**

Cassy Pear

Cassy Pear

REAL PROPERTIES, INC., a corporation

BY *Diane Holst, President*

BY *James Holst, Secretary*

RECORDING REQUESTED BY

TITLE COMPANY

AND WHEN RECORDED MAIL TO

REAL PROPERTIES, INC.
P.O. Box 682
Berkeley CA 94702

SEP 20 1984
84 137602

RECORDED AT REQUEST OF
BOOK 11983 PAGE 202
TITLE COMPANY
OF CONTRA COSTA

OFFICIAL RECORDS OF
CONTRA COSTA COUNTY

CONTRA COSTA CO
TRANSFER TAX
22.55

COUNTY RECORDER

SURVEY
MONUMENT
FUND
$10

SPACE ABOVE FOR RECORDER'S USE ONLY

MAIL TAX STATEMENTS TO

NO CHANGE

COUNTY MONUMENT USER FEE $10.00

DOCUMENTARY TRANSFER TAX $ 22.55

COMPUTED ON FULL VALUE OF
PROPERTY CONVEYED, OR
COMPUTED ON FULL VALUE
LESS LIENS & ENCUMBRANCES REMAIN-
ING THEREON AT TIME OF SALE.

AS DECLARED BY THE UNDERSIGNED

A.P.N.: 527-012-002
Order No. 49333
Escrow No.

GRANT DEED

Signature of declarant or agent determining tax

DAVID MACLEAN, an unmarried man

(GRANTOR · GRANTORS)

FOR A VALUABLE CONSIDERATION, receipt of which is hereby acknowledged,
Do es Hereby Grant To

REAL PROPERTIES, INC., a corporation

the real property in the   City of Richmond
County of   Contra Costa   , State of California, described as follows

FOR LEGAL DESCRIPTION SEE EXHIBIT "A" ATTACHED HERETO

Dated   9/17/84

STATE OF CALIFORNIA
COUNTY OF
CONTRA COSTA   } SS

On   September 19, 1984
before me, the undersigned, a Notary Public in and for said
County and State, personally appeared
David Maclean

known to me (or proved to me on the basis of satisfactory
evidence) to be the same person whose name   is

subscribed to the within instrument, and acknowledged to
me that   he   executed the same.
WITNESS my hand and official seal.

Notary's signature Cassy Pear

David Maclean
David Maclean

FOR NOTARY STAMP OR SEAL

OFFICIAL Seal
CASSY PEAR
NOTARY PUBLIC-CALIFORNIA
CONTRA COSTA COUNTY
My Commission Expires May 26, 1987

CCPH

Order No 49333 PC

вис 11983 гки 208

EXHIBIT "A" as referred to in the deed of trust dated 9/17/84
REAL PROPERTIES, INC., to trustee a: ' David McLean beneficiary

The land referred to in this Report is situated in the State of California, County of Contra Costa
City of Richmond   and is described as follows:

Portion of Lots 11 and 13, Block 19, map of the San Pablo Villa Tract, filed September
21, 1905, Map Book C, page 65, Contra Costa County Records, described as follows:

Beginning on the east line of Hayes Street, formerly Powell Street, distant thereon
north 0 degrees 45' west 59 feet from the southwest corner of said Block 19; thence
from said point of beginning north 0 degrees 45' east along the east line of Hayes
Street 41.5 feet; thence southeasterly parallel with the south line of Emeric Avenue,
formerly Clay Street 112.5 feet to the west line of Lot 12; thence southerly along
said line 41.5 feet; thence northwesterly parallel with the south line of Emeric
Avenue 112.5 feet to the point of beginning.

Order No. 49333 PC

EXHIBIT "A" AS REFERRED TO IN THE DEED FROM DAVID MACLEAN TO REAL PROPERTIES, INC., a California corporation dated 9/17/84

The land referred to in this Report is situated in the State of California, County of Contra Costa and is described as follows:

City of Richmond

Portion of Lots 11 and 13, Block 19, map of the San Pablo Villa Tract, filed September 21, 1905, Map Book C, page 65, Contra Costa County Records, described as follows:

Beginning on the east line of Mayes Street, formerly Powell Street, distant thereon north 0 degrees 45' west 59 feet from the southwest corner of said Block 19; thence from said point of beginning north 0 degrees 45' east along the east line of Mayes Street 41.5 feet; thence southeasterly parallel with the south line of Emeric Avenue, formerly Clay Street 112.5 feet to the west line of Lot 12; thence southerly along said line 41.5 feet; thence northwesterly parallel with the south line of Emeric Avenue 112.5 feet to the point of beginning.

SCHEDULE A
CLTA Preliminary Report
1-1-84

Page 2 of 2

TITLE
GUARANTY COMPANY

11983 209

"Exhibit A" to Deed of Trust

~~This Note shall have a prepayment prepayment allocated to payor the payment shall be shown in~~
~~waive however to the extent... failure to make such periodic payments shall not be a~~
~~default of this Note. Unpaid payments shall not be added to principal and shall accumulate and be paid in full with the~~
~~final payment of the Note.~~

Payor has the option of making a prepayment of several monthly installments (minimum six installments). By doing so,
the payor may discount the total sum of the actual payments by __10__ per cent and the resulting amount be paid in
lieu of the total sum of the actual scheduled installment payments due for that period. Said prepayment shall waive
installment payments for the same number of months after the payments were prepaid. This Note to have no prepayment
penalty if paid in full or in part before the due date. Payor may at any time within __60__ months of the date of
this Note prepay the entire Note and may discount the then due principal balance by __10__ per cent.

At the time this Note is due and payable, Note Holder agrees to extend the due date for an additional twelve months, if
payor agrees to change the interest rate to 2% over the Federal Discount Rate.

~~The Note Holder agrees to allow future subordination of collateral to the taxes another property can be one they~~
~~accrue... Note Holder shall release the lien against the property whereby securing the Note and~~
~~... Note Holder the sum of the... the subscription of~~
~~additional including the unpaid principal and interest of this Note shall not exceed... the value~~
~~... as determined appraised of the other property~~

~~The Note Holder agrees to subordinate... the any new financing and/or the Notes and Deeds~~
~~of... any additional... the senior loans shall have an interest rate... and the keep... the area... at... such a adequate not exceed that new~~
~~year... the due date of this Note... the Note Holder, the such of... allowing the... including... shall not exceed eighty... except... the value as x"~~
~~... by... appraised of property~~

Should the Note Holder decide to sell this Note, the Note Holder must first offer it to the payor. The payor may
purchase it within 30 days. The payor shall also have 30 days to match any bona fide written offer received at a later
time from a third party.

The obligation for the payment of this Note and Deed of Trust can be assumed by another party at any time in the future
retaining the same terms and conditions.

The liability of this Note shall be limited to the property itself, and shall not extend beyond it. The payor shall
have no personal liability. This Note is given as a portion of the purchase price of real property and any Note Holder
hereof shall accept the Note subject to any and all claims arising out of the purchase transaction.

IAS Form 101-B Revision 9.13 Copyright 1984

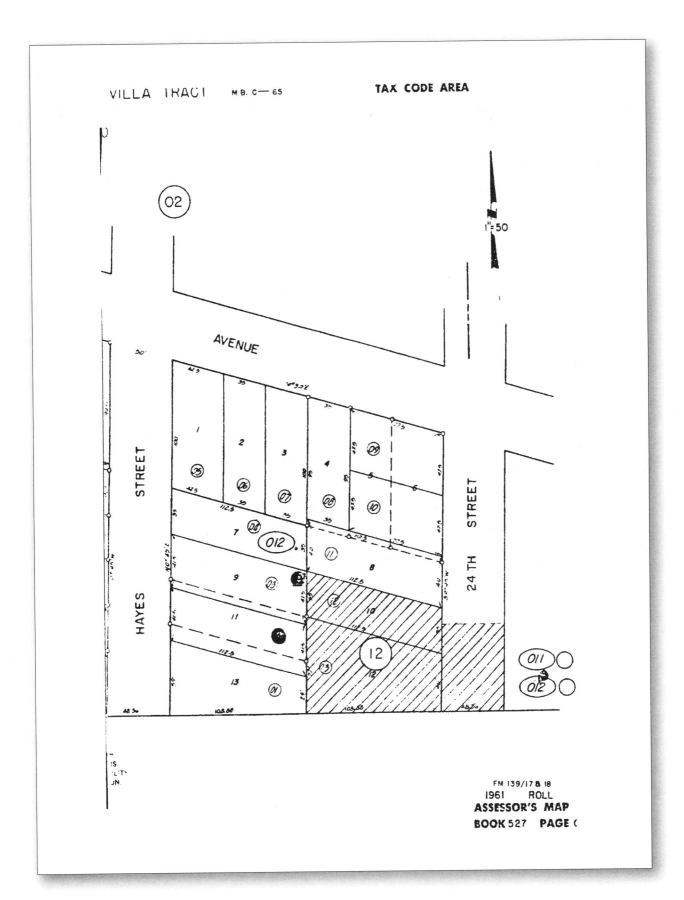

ORDER NO.

he land referred to in this Report is situated in the State of California, County of Marin
nd is described as follows:

LOT 195, as shown upon that certain map entitled, "Map of Greenbrae Sub.
No. One, Marin Co. Calif.", filed May 2, 1946 in Book 6 of Maps, at Page
7, Marin County Records.

t the date hereof exceptions to coverage in addition to the Exceptions and Exclusions in said policy form would be as
ollows:

1. Taxes, general and special, for the fiscal year 1984&85, a lien
not yet due or payable.

2. The lien of Supplemental Taxes assessed pursuant to Chapter 498,
Statutes of 1983 of the State of California.

3. Taxes, general and special, for the fiscal year 1983&84, as follows:

Assessor's Parcel No.: 70-192-11
Code No.   : 68-004

1st Installment   : $371.19 Paid
2nd Installment   : $371.19 Delinquent
                      37.11 Penalty
Land   : $24,960
Improvement Value   : $40,210
Personal Prop. Value : $NONE
Exemption   : $7000 - Householder

"Any amounts which may be added to the Property Tax amounts by reason of
a Reappraisal of any improvements added to, or change of Ownership of,
the herein described Premises subsequent to March 1, 1975".

Chapter 2

Who Must Sign the Deed?

One important question you must answer before you transfer title to real property is whether you can do it by yourself or whether you need someone else's cooperation. The basic rule is simple: If someone else appears to have, for any legitimate reason, a claim to an ownership interest in the property being transferred, you should not try to transfer title unless that person either gives up that claim (by signing a quitclaim deed to you) or signs the transfer deed along with you. Otherwise, your transfer will be incomplete—you can only transfer what you own.

The consequences of an incomplete or confused transfer are unhappy. First of all, the person receiving the property gets less than appears in the transfer deed. And when the deed recognizing the botched or incomplete transfer is recorded, the public record of ownership will be wrong. This can make it difficult, later, to sell the property or borrow money on it. The point is that you want to be sure about who owns the property being transferred and that each owner signs the deed.

Exceptions, exceptions: Like almost all good advice, the admonition to have all owners sign the deed doesn't always apply. In a few instances it may make sense for you to transfer your part interest in real property, if the new owner clearly understands that you have only a part interest in it. For example, if you own land with two siblings, you may want to go ahead and transfer your interest to your brother and let him deal with your sister about getting her to make a similar transfer.

You don't need to get anyone else to participate in the transfer of a piece of real property, if you are in one of these four common situations:

- You are married, both you and your spouse are willing to sign the deed, and there are no other co-owners.
- You are single, not living with anyone, and are the sole owner of the property.
- All co-owners of the property agree to the transfer or the change in the way title is held (for example, from tenancy in common to joint tenancy) and all will sign the deed (with their spouses, if any are married), or

- The property is owned in the name of a partnership, and all partners are willing to sign the deed.

If you are in one of these categories, you can safely transfer your property by yourself and skip the rest of this chapter. This means if you want to sell or give away property, or put it in a living trust, you can go directly to Chapter 3. If you want to make property security for a loan and execute a trust deed, go to Chapter 4 instead.

If you don't fit in one of these four categories, it means you need more information before you make your transfer. The rest of this chapter shows you how to proceed.

Transfers From Married Persons or Domestic Partners

The basic rule of transfers from married persons is that both spouses must sign the deed. Whether the property is in both names (held as community property, joint tenancy, or tenancy in common) or only in the name of one spouse, both should sign.

The same rules apply to registered domestic partners.

Spouses of all co-owners should sign. For example, if two brothers, Phillip and Charles, want to transfer some land they own together, both Phillip and Charles and their wives should sign the deed.

It's easy to understand why you need the signature of both spouses or domestic partners if both names are on the existing deed. But why do you need two signatures if the property is in one person's name and belongs to him as separate property? The answer lies in California's community property laws. California law regards most property acquired by a married person or domestic partner as community property—that is, it belongs to the couple as a unit, not to either person separately. Both must jointly make any transfer or encumbrance of community real property. (Fam. Code § 1102. Transfers made by one spouse, if title is held in the name of that spouse only, may be challenged in court for up to a year after the deed is recorded in the county recorder's office.) And because separate property owned by one spouse can easily be turned (at least partially) into community property (very easily if, for example, community property funds are used to improve it, pay taxes on it, or make payments on a mortgage), in practice both spouses must usually sign before any real property owned by a married person can be transferred or mortgaged.

The point, and it's an important one, is that there's usually no reliable way for a third party to know whether under the law a married person or registered domestic partner really owns a piece of real property all by himself. For that reason, banks and escrow companies always insist that both spouses sign deeds and other documents involved in property transfers. Having both spouses sign the deed instantly and easily eliminates any doubts about the completeness of the transfer, and no one has to worry about whether or not the property was separate or community.

Remember that even if a bank or title insurer isn't involved in the current transfer, one or both will almost certainly be in on some subsequent sale and will insist on a title search then. If it is found that a prior transfer was made by one spouse without the signature of the other, the bank, or a title insurance company the bank depends on, may not approve the new proposed transfer.

What if you something prevents your spouse from joining in the transfer of title to property that you are convinced is yours alone? You can make the transfer without the signature of your spouse if you are sure that the property is your separate property and others would readily draw the same conclusion. To make this determination, you must take the time to become familiar with California community property laws. Here are some rules of thumb.

In general, real estate is probably all or partially community property if:

- the property was acquired during the marriage with money earned by either spouse or domestic partner after marriage
- both your names appear on the deed
- your spouse has contributed a significant amount of time or labor to the property's improvement, or

- community funds were used for improvements, taxes, or mortgage payments. (Community funds are, in general, any funds acquired by either spouse during the marriage except those acquired by one spouse only by gift or inheritance.)

In a few instances, however, property belongs entirely to one spouse alone (separate property) and can be transferred without the other's consent. To be separate property, the real estate must pass two tests. First, it must have been:

- owned and paid for by one spouse before the marriage
- given to one spouse as a gift
- inherited by one spouse
- paid for totally with one spouse's separate property, or
- acquired after the spouses permanently separated.

Second, no community property funds can have been spent on improvements, taxes, or mortgage payments for the property.

If, for example, you purchased the property with your separate property money, you never used your earnings or other community funds to make improvements or pay the mortgage or taxes, and title is held in your name alone, it will qualify as your separate property. If so, you can legally transfer it without your spouse's signature. To repeat an important point, if a bank or escrow company is involved, it will probably be conservative on this point and insist on your spouse's signature no matter how persuasively you argue that your real estate isn't community property.

If after reading this you are sure the real estate is your separate property, and there is some problem with obtaining your spouse's signature, you can go ahead and transfer title to the property with only your signature on the deed. But again, remember that there may be problems down the road when the new owner goes to transfer title, because it may not be clear to a third party that your spouse had no claim to the property.

What About Living Together?

In a few instances, you may need the signature of the person you live with even if you aren't married or in a registered domestic partnership. Since the California Supreme Court's 1976 decision in the Lee Marvin-Michele Triola Marvin "palimony" case, it's possible that a "significant other" may have a claim to property you acquire while living together.

In the *Marvin* case, the court found that the couple had an implied contract (that is, a mutual understanding that wasn't explicitly stated or written down) to share property ownership. Because California courts recognize such implied contracts, if they can be proved, some members of unmarried couples undoubtedly have ownership interests in the property held in the names of their friends (or ex-friends). If you think your friend may sometime press a claim against property you want to transfer, play it safe. Talk the situation over. If you reach an amicable understanding, get a quitclaim deed from him before the transfer.

Transfers from Unmarried Co-Owners

This chapter is divided along marriage lines because of the enormous importance of California's community property laws any time you transfer real property. This section deals only with transactions where all owners who want to transfer property are unmarried and are not registered domestic partners.

If all co-owners of the property agree to the transfer or the change in the way title is held (for example, from tenancy in common to joint tenancy) and all will sign the deed, you can go directly to Chapter 3, which discusses how the new owners should take title. If a co-owner wants to transfer his interest on his own, read on.

To know your rights when you are a co-owner of real property, you must know in what form you hold title. You are either a "joint tenant," a "tenant in common," or a partner. Although co-owners are sometimes referred to as "tenants" ("tenants in common" or "joint tenants"), this doesn't mean they're renting the property. It's just another archaic legal term that, unfortunately, is impossible to avoid.

To find out how you and your co-owners hold title, consult the deed that gave you title to the property. It will probably specify that you and your co-owners hold title either "as joint tenants," "as tenants in common," or in the name of the partnership. Joint tenancy is also sometimes indicated by the form "to John and Claudia with right of survivorship." If it doesn't say, you are tenants in common, unless the property was bought with partnership funds (in which case the partnership owns the property). If you received your interest in the land from someone who was a part-owner (someone who didn't own the whole property), you are a tenant in common. Thus if your deed transferred to you "a half interest in the following property…" you are a tenant in common.

Partitions

Sometimes one co-owner wants to split the property, but the other co-owners won't agree to it. In that case, one owner may request that a court in the county where the land is located either split the property or order it sold and the proceeds split. That process is called a partition.

Every co-owner has an absolute right to obtain a partition of the property. No particular reason is necessary. The court usually orders that the property be sold and the proceeds divided among the owners according to their ownership interests. The court can, however, order that the property be physically divided. To file a partition action, you'll need a lawyer's advice.

Recording requested by
　John and Claudia O'Huffell
　78 Sherwood Drive
　Oakland, CA 94718

and when recorded mail
this deed and tax statements to
　same as above

For recorder's use

Grant Deed

☑ This transfer is exempt from the documentary transfer tax.

☐ The documentary transfer tax is $_____ and is computed on:

　☐ the full value of the interest or property conveyed.

　☐ the full value less the value of liens or encumbrances remaining thereon at the time of sale.

The property is located in ☐ an unincorporated area. ☑ the city of ___Oakland_____

For a valuable consideration, receipt of which is hereby acknowledged, __John O'Huffell or Claudia O'Huffell__

_____ hereby grant(s) to __John O'Huffell or__

__Claudia O'Huffell, as joint tenants,_____

the following real property in the City of ___Oakland___, County of ___Alameda___ California:

Tenants in Common

As an unmarried tenant in common, you are free to do just about whatever you want with your interest in commonly owned property. If you want to get rid of your interest, you may sell it, give it away, or leave it in your will, just like any other property you own alone.

Because tenants in common own "undivided interests" in the property, each can sell only that interest, not a specific part of the property. If, for example, Joanne and her brother Ed own half interests in a ten-acre piece of property as tenants in common, Joanne is free to sell her interest in the property to her friend Jillian. Ed can't stop her. Only Joanne needs to sign the deed.

Joanne, however, cannot sell five acres of the land; she can only transfer her half-interest in the whole property. That's what her friend Jillian would get: a half-interest in the entire ten acres.

If co-owners want to split up the property, they need to execute two deeds, each transferring half the property. Remember that zoning laws often restrict how property may be divided. Check with your city or county planning department before you start carving up your land. If the property is on the coast, you probably also need approval from the California Coastal Commission.

Joint Tenants

If you hold title to real property in joint tenancy (discussed in Chapter 3), you can easily transfer your interest in the property, whether or not the other joint tenants agree to or even know of the change.

Transferring Your Interest in the Property

The simplest way to end the joint tenancy is to execute and record a deed transferring your interest to yourself, or anyone else, as a tenant in common. (Civ. Code § 683.2.) That destroys the joint tenancy as to your interest. The deed usually must be recorded (filed in the county recorder's office) before your death to defeat the survivorship interests of the remaining joint tenants. (See Chapter 6.) To transfer your interest in the property (now held as a tenancy in common), you need only sign the deed yourself.

> **EXAMPLE:** Jesse and his sister, Angie, own their house as joint tenants. Without telling Angie, Jesse executes a deed transferring his interest from himself as a joint tenant to himself as a tenant in common.

This severs the joint tenancy, as long as the deed is recorded before Jesse's death. Jesse and Angie become tenants in common. Upon either's death, his or her half-interest will pass to beneficiaries under a will or heirs, not to the surviving joint tenant (again, the characteristics of joint tenancy are set out in detail in Chapter 3).

Suppose now that there are more than two joint tenants. If one executes a deed to herself as a tenant in common, she will then be a tenant in common with the other two co-tenants, who remain joint tenants with respect to their two-thirds interest in the property. Joint tenancy rules govern the relationship between the two joint tenants, while tenancy in common rules apply to relations between the joint tenants and the tenant in common.

Recording requested by
Jesse M. Costa
937 Livermore Ave.
Danville, CA 94558

and when recorded mail
this deed and tax statements to

Same as above

For recorder's use

Grant Deed

☑ This transfer is exempt from the documentary transfer tax.

☐ The documentary transfer tax is $_____ and is computed on:

   ☐ the full value of the interest or property conveyed.

   ☐ the full value less the value of liens or encumbrances remaining thereon at the time of sale.

The property is located in ☐ an unincorporated area. ☑ the city of _____Danville_____

For a valuable consideration, receipt of which is hereby acknowledged, _____Jesse M. Costa, joint tenant,_____

_____ hereby grant(s) to _Jesse M. Costa,_

as a tenant in common, a one-half interest in

the following real property in the City of _____Danville_____, County of _____Contra Costa_____ California:

EXAMPLE: Marsha, Joe, and Helen own a piece of property as joint tenants. Marsha sells her one-third interest to Dan. Dan does not become a joint tenant. He is a tenant in common with Joe and Helen. He is free to leave his interest in the property through his will (or put it into a living trust); if he doesn't have a will (or trust), it will pass to his heirs under state law. Joe and Helen are not entitled to receive it when Dan dies, and Dan will not receive their interests when they die. Joe and Helen, however, remain joint tenants as between themselves.

Executing a Deed of Trust

If you're a joint tenant you may sign a deed of trust yourself, making your interest in the property security for a loan. This does *not* terminate the joint tenancy. However, if a creditor forecloses on the property and a joint tenant's interest is sold, the sale terminates the joint tenancy (as between the buyer of the interest and the other joint tenant(s)) in the same way that a voluntary transfer would.

Transfers by Surviving Joint Tenants

A deceased joint tenant's interest in property passes to the surviving joint tenants, who record an affidavit with the county recorder giving notice of the joint tenant's death. (The procedure is set out in Julia Nissley's *How to Probate an Estate in California* (Nolo).) If, later on, the surviving joint tenants want to transfer title to the property, they should sign the deed as "surviving joint tenants."

Transfers of Partnership Property

Real property is often held in the name of a partnership, an entity formed by two or more people to conduct a business. The transfer rules are governed by the partnership agreement or, if the agreement doesn't cover it, the Uniform Partnership Act (UPA). (Corp. Code § 16100 and following.) Under the UPA, any partner may transfer real property held in the partnership name if the transfer is apparently for carrying on the business of the partnership, unless:

- the partner in fact doesn't have authority to make the particular transfer, and
- the person with whom the partner deals knows the partner doesn't have the authority.

If the partnership agreement limits certain partners' authority to transfer real property, the partnership should record the agreement in any county where the partnership owns real property. Once it's recorded, it gives notice to all prospective purchasers that only certain partners can transfer partnership real property. Check the partnership agreement for restrictions and rules about how the transfer can be made.

EXAMPLE 1: Brian and Fred run a real estate business as partners. Their partnership agreement doesn't say anything about transferring the partnership's property. Under the UPA, either may sign a deed to transfer partnership property or subject it to a deed of trust.

EXAMPLE 2: Fred wants to borrow money because he sunk all his savings in the partnership. He wants to sign a deed of trust giving the partnership's real property as security for a loan. Under the UPA (and most partnership agreements), he can't unless Brian agrees and signs, too, because this isn't in the course of partnership business.

Further, most partnership agreements restrict your freedom to transfer only your interest in the partnership property. Usually, the other partners get a chance to buy out your interest before you can sell it.

EXAMPLE: Jane decides she wants out of the partnership she, Jeremy, and Ruth have, and decides to try to sell her interest in the partnership's real property. Under the terms of the partnership agreement, she must first offer to sell her interest to Ruth and Jeremy.

Partnership information. For a thorough discussion of partnership agreements, see *Form a Partnership: The Complete Legal Guide,* by Denis Clifford and Ralph Warner (Nolo).

Transfers of Corporate Property

Corporations are governed by special rules about how real property transfers can be made and who is authorized to make them. Generally, the board of directors must approve, by resolution, sale of corporate assets. The deed is signed by an officer of the corporation who is authorized by the board to sell property, and the corporate seal is embossed on the deed. If a transfer is made to liquidate the corporation's assets (not in the course of the corporation's business), shareholder approval may be required. Before you transfer corporate property, check the California Corporations Code.

More on corporations. For information on how to adopt corporate resolutions, see *The Corporate Records Handbook: Meetings, Minutes & Resolutions,* by Anthony Mancuso (Nolo).

Transfers of Limited Liability Company Property

The owners (members) of a limited liability company (LLC) must approve the purchase or sale of real estate by the company. You'll want to pass a formal resolution approving the transaction, and have a member with the necessary authority sign the deed on behalf of the LLC.

LLC real estate. *Your Limited Liability Company: An Operating Manual,* by Anthony Mancuso (Nolo), explains how to approve real estate transfers and prepare the necessary paperwork to document your decisions.

Transfers From Trustees

Trusts are designed to hold property (in the name of a trustee) for someone (the beneficiary) for a certain period of time. It's common, for example, to put property in trust for a child.

As discussed in Chapter 3, property must be formally transferred, with a grant deed, to the trustee. When the time comes to transfer the property from the trust back to an outright owner (either the person who set up the trust, if the trust is being revoked, or the named beneficiary), another formal transfer, with a deed, is necessary. The trustee must sign the deed, which would look like the example below.

Owners Who Can't Sign a Deed

Not everyone who owns real property is free to transfer it. In certain narrow circumstances, a property owner may lack the legal capacity to execute a deed, and someone with proper legal standing must sign for the actual owner. The two most common situations are when a minor owns property or a property owner is mentally incompetent.

Minors

A minor (in California, someone less than 18 years old) may not make a valid deed. Any deed signed by a minor is void and has no effect. The minor's guardian (in most cases, someone approved by the probate court, because minors usually acquire real property by inheritance) must sign the deed.

The one exception is a minor who is emancipated —that is, one who has been married, is in the military, or who has received a decree of emancipation from a court. (Fam. Code § 7050.) An emancipated minor has the same rights as an adult when it comes to owning property.

Recording requested by
    David R. Maclean
    665 Newman Street
    St. Helena, CA 94573

and when recorded mail
this deed and tax statements to
    Same as above

For recorder's use

Grant Deed

☑ This transfer is exempt from the documentary transfer tax.

☐ The documentary transfer tax is $_____ and is computed on:

    ☐ the full value of the interest or property conveyed.

    ☐ the full value less the value of liens or encumbrances remaining thereon at the time of sale.

The property is located in ☐ an unincorporated area. ☑ the city of ___St. Helena___

For a valuable consideration, receipt of which is hereby acknowledged, __Marjorie Simmons, Trustee of the__ ___David R. Maclean Revocable Living Trust___ hereby grant(s) to ___David R. Maclean___

the following real property in the City of _____St. Helena_____, County of _____Napa_____ California:

Persons With Mental Impairment

All that is required of a person executing a deed, as far as mental capacity is concerned, is the ability to understand the nature of the transaction and its consequences. Old age, ill health, or some mental impairment does not automatically render a deed suspect.

If, however, a court has determined that someone is of unsound mind, that person may not transfer property. Any deed signed by such a person is void. (Civ. Code §§ 38, 40.)

To complicate things further, there is another category of questionable deeds. If a deed is executed by a person "of unsound mind, but not entirely without understanding" who has not been judicially determined to be of unsound mind, the deed is not automatically void. It is, however, voidable by the grantor—that is, the grantor can change his mind later and bring a lawsuit to get the property back. (Civ. Code § 39.) Most often, such actions are brought by a conservator who is later appointed to manage the person's affairs.

EXAMPLE: Florence, an elderly woman, transfers her house to her nephew. A few months later, a court rules that she is incompetent, and a conservator is appointed for her. The conservator may sue the nephew on the ground that Florence was not of sound mind when she executed the deed. If the conservator wins, the court will rescind the deed, giving the property back to Florence.

Don't take chances. If you think a deed may be challenged later based on the mental capacity of the person who signs it, see an attorney.

Persons Who Have Executed a Power of Attorney

Giving someone the "power of attorney" gives that person the power to take certain actions on your behalf. The person you appoint is called your "attorney-in-fact" or "agent."

Power of attorney must be given in writing. When it gives someone authority to transfer or encumber real estate, it should also be recorded with the county recorder. If there is no written record that the person who signs the deed was in fact authorized to do so, the chain of title will have a gap in it.

> **EXAMPLE:** Sara signs a power of attorney that gives Ellen authority to act for her in all legal matters while she is in Europe for six months. This authorization includes signing a deed to the house Ellen and Sara co-own and are trying to sell. If they don't record the power of attorney with the county recorder in the county where the property is located, a subsequent title search would show that only Ellen signed the deed to the house. Without a record of the written authorization, the deed would appear ineffective to transfer Sara's interest in the property.

An attorney-in-fact must specify that he is acting for the owner of the property by signing the deed, for example, "Ellen Palmer, attorney-in-fact for Sara Puchinsky."

Two kinds of powers of attorney are useful for property transfers:

- A conventional power of attorney gives the attorney-in-fact authority to act in specific matters or for a specific period of time, when someone will be temporarily unable to take care of legal matters (for example, because he will be out of the country).

- A durable power of attorney is used when you want to ensure that if you should become incapacitated, a person you trust will be empowered to make important decisions about your medical treatment or business affairs. Unlike a conventional power of attorney, it does not automatically end if the person becomes incapacitated.

Chapter 3

How Should the New Owners Take Title?

*A*fter you've cleared up the question of who must sign the deed to transfer your property (Chapter 2), it's time to look at the other end of the transaction and decide how the recipients should take title to the property. You can't prepare a deed until you figure out how to specify the way title will be held by the new owners.

Transfers to One Unmarried Recipient

If you're transferring property to one person who is neither married nor in a registered domestic partnership, consider yourself lucky. You don't need to worry about choosing the form of the new owner's title; simply put down the recipient's name.

It's a good idea to point out on the deed itself that the recipient is unmarried, just so no one later has to wonder whether a spouse had a community property interest in the property transferred. Thus a deed to an unmarried woman would state, for example, that the current owner grants the property "to Elizabeth H. Bernstein, an unmarried woman."

More Than One Unmarried Recipient

Unmarried persons to whom title is being transferred jointly may take title in one of three forms: a tenancy in common, joint tenancy, or partnership (in the partnership's name). (Unmarried couples who have registered with the state as domestic partners have the same choices as married couples, discussed below.) This choice can have significant consequences when:

- the interest of a co-owner is later sold
- the interests of all owners are sold at the same time, or
- a co-owner dies.

Unless the new owners are already in or want to form a partnership—two or more persons who own a business together—they will want to take title as joint tenants or tenants in common. Partnerships are discussed later in this chapter.

Shared Features of Joint Tenancy and Tenancy in Common

Tenancy in common and joint tenancy, the most common forms of co-ownership, share many features, including:

- **Equal right to use or sell the property.** No matter what shares joint owners have in real property, no co-owner has the exclusive right to use or transfer a specific physical part of the property. Instead, each co-owner has, in legal jargon, an "undivided interest" in the property. Each may use the whole property and each is entitled to income from the whole property in proportion to his ownership share. For example, if three joint tenants (who always own equal shares) own a farm that is leased for $30,000 a year, each is entitled to $10,000.

  In other words, if you own property as a joint tenant or tenant in common, you do not own a particular, physically defined half of the property. You may transfer only your particular share of the overall ownership.

EXAMPLE: Joanne and Ed Fisher, brother and sister, each own a one-half interest in a ten-acre mountain lot they inherited from their parents. Informally, they agree that Ed will live on the south half of the property while Joanne will occupy the north half. Both Ed and Joanne build cabins on their portions. Later, Ed and Joanne have a feud and decide that ten acres is too small for the two of them. Neither wishes to buy the other out. Joanne simply wants to sell her portion of the land and move to New York. Can she sell just five acres? No. Despite their arrangement, neither Ed nor Joanne owns a five-acre piece. Thus, Joanne can sell only her one-half interest in the ten acres as a whole (but see the discussion below on partitions).

Because co-owners are entitled to their proportionate share of income from the property, if Ed rented out his cabin three months a year for $200 a month, Joanne would be entitled to

$300 (half of $600). If Ed owned a 90% interest in the property, his share of the income would be $540 (90% of $600). As co-owners, Ed and Joanne are also responsible for their proportionate shares of expenses, including taxes, repairs and maintenance, and insurance. If Joanne pays more than her share of these costs, she is entitled to reimbursement from Ed. Similarly, if she damages the property, she must reimburse Ed for the reduction in market value of his interest.

- **Right to partition.** If one co-owner is unable to sell just his separate interest (as is often the case) and the co-owners can't agree on selling or dividing the property, any of them may request a partition from a court in the county where the land is located. (See Chapter 2.)

When to Use Tenancy in Common

Tenancy in common is the appropriate form of ownership for most co-owners unless they already have a close family relationship (in that case joint tenancy—discussed below—may be more appropriate). Generally speaking, it is necessary to create a tenancy in common when:

- the new co-owners want to leave their interests in the property to someone other than their fellow co-owner(s), or
- the new co-owners want to own the property in unequal shares (for example, one co-owner owns a two-thirds interest and another owns one-third).

A big drawback to owning real property in tenancy in common has always been the necessity for probate when a co-owner dies. Probate can be avoided if the property is in a living trust or held in joint tenancy.

In California, any transfer of real property to two or more persons automatically creates a tenancy in common unless the deed says otherwise. No special words are necessary. This deed language would create a tenancy in common:

"to Darrell Buckner, Len Ryan, and Roberta Fernandez, as tenants in common."

So would this:

"to Nolan Gooden and Dwight Wilson."

When to Use Joint Tenancy

Joint tenancy, although useful in many situations, reduces the flexibility that a joint owner has in respect to his property interest. It is generally advisable for unmarried persons who:

- want the property to automatically (without probate) go to the surviving co-owners upon a co-owner's death, and
- want each joint owner to own an equal share of the property.

Probably the most significant feature of joint tenancy is that when one joint tenant dies, his interest in the property goes to the surviving joint tenants, even if his will contains a provision to the contrary. Probate proceedings are not necessary to effect the transfer, which can therefore be accomplished quickly and easily. For this reason, joint tenancy is often used by persons in a close, long-term personal relationship.

Joint tenancy is not always the best way to avoid probate. Take the common situation of an older person who wants to keep control of property during her lifetime, have it go to a child or other younger relative at her death, and avoid probate. She can accomplish most of these goals by putting the property in joint tenancy with the younger relative. The drawback is that she can't change her mind and take the property back once someone else's name is on the title. If, like King Lear, she is later confronted by an ungrateful child, thinks better of her generosity, and wants the land back, she will find that she can't take back the gift. If, on the other hand, she put the property in a living trust (which would also avoid probate), naming her relative as beneficiary, she could at any time change the terms of the trust or terminate it altogether. (A living trust could have saved Lear a lot of trouble.)

Joint tenants must own equal shares; you cannot create a joint tenancy in which one person owns, for example, a two-thirds interest in the property.

To create a joint tenancy, a deed must specify that the co-tenants hold title as joint tenants or "with right of survivorship." The deed need not be titled "Joint Tenancy Deed" (though some are) as long as it designates the new owners as joint tenants.

> **EXAMPLE:** Below is what a deed from Joanne and Ed (from our earlier example) would look like if they wanted to become joint tenants.

Tax Note: Although joint tenancy can be used to avoid probate, it will not avoid federal estate taxes.

All property in which a decedent had any interest, including joint tenancy property that passes outside probate, is counted for federal estate tax purposes. (See Chapter 1.)

Joint tenancy and estate taxes. These issues are discussed in more detail in *Plan Your Estate*, by Denis Clifford and Cora Jordan, and *How to Probate an Estate in California*, by Julia Nissley (both from Nolo).

Ask an expert. If you are not sure, after reading this section, how the new owners should take title, see a knowledgeable real estate professional or attorney. See Chapter 7 for a discussion of how to find and work with one.

Recording requested by
  Joanne Hayden
  Edward Hayden
  3645 Eagle Creek Road
  Palmdale, CA 97329
and when recorded mail
this deed and tax statements to

  Same as above

                              For recorder's use

Grant Deed

☑ This transfer is exempt from the documentary transfer tax.

☐ The documentary transfer tax is $_____ and is computed on:

    ☐ the full value of the interest or property conveyed.

    ☐ the full value less the value of liens or encumbrances remaining thereon at the time of sale.

The property is located in ☑ an unincorporated area. ☐ the city of _____

For a valuable consideration, receipt of which is hereby acknowledged, <u>Joanne Hayden and Edward Hayden,</u>

<u>tenants in common,</u> hereby grant(s) to <u>Joanne Hayden and</u>

<u>Edward Hayden, as joint tenants,</u>

the following real property in the ~~City of~~ xxxxxxxxxxxxxxxxxxxxxx , County of _____Kern_____ California:

Changing the Terms of Co-ownership by Contract

If co-owners are unhappy with the terms of the co-ownership—if, for example, they don't want to own "undivided interests" in the property, they can partition the property, either by simply executing new deeds or going to court. For example, Ed and Joanne could execute two deeds, each giving one of them five acres of the property. (This would, however, necessitate having a surveyor draw up new legal descriptions of the property for the two deeds. Division of property is often also limited by local zoning laws.)

In some special situations, however, co-owners may not want to divide the property. Instead, they may want to make a separate agreement among themselves about the use of the property. For example, in some cities, restrictions on converting rental property to condominiums (that is, separate ownership of each unit) make it impossible for co-owners to divide ownership of a duplex or fourplex. The co-owners could, however, make a contract that gives each owner specific rights to use a certain part of the jointly owned property.

Such contracts can be quite complicated, and local zoning ordinances and state laws may restrict their content. Before you make one, see a real estate attorney.

Transfers to Married Recipients

Married persons have several choices of how to take title to real property. Like unmarried co-owners, married couples may take title as joint tenants or tenants in common (discussed above). Or one person could hold title separately. Most married couples, however, will want to specify on the deed that the property is being held "as community property with right of survivorship."

Domestic partners: California's community property laws apply to domestic partners who have registered with the state, in exactly the way they apply to married couples.

Advantages of Community Property With Right of Survivorship

This form of ownership allows survivors to avoid probate and offers a tax planning advantage as well.

Probate Avoidance

Property held as community property with right of survivorship goes directly to a surviving spouse or domestic partner without having to pass through probate. The survivor need only record a simple document with the county recorder. This avoids not only lengthy delays in transferring title into the name of the survivor, but also probate fees.

 If you don't want to leave the property to your spouse or partner, hold title in a different way. If you and your spouse or partner own the property as "community property with right of survivorship," at your death your spouse or partner will inherit your half—even if your will contains instructions to the contrary. If you want the other advantages of community property without the automatic right of survivorship, you can hold title as plain "community property."

Tax Planning

If you own property that has gone up a great deal in value since you acquired it, holding title as community property can make it easier for a surviving spouse who inherits the property to qualify for special federal income tax treatment. (This tax benefit does not apply to domestic partners, who may not file federal taxes as spouses.) It still may be possible to qualify for this treatment when the property is not designated as community property on the deed, but it's more difficult.

Checklist for Real Property Transfers				
	Tenancy in Common	**Joint Tenancy**	**Partnership**	**Community Property**	**Community Property With Right of Survivorship**
Creation	Deed must transfer property to two or more persons "as tenants in common" or without specifying how title is to be held.	Deed must transfer property to two or more persons "as joint tenants" or "with right of survivorship."	Deed must transfer property to the name of the partnership, or partnership funds must be used to buy it.	Deed must transfer property to a married couple or domestic partners "as community property" or "as husband and wife."	Deed must transfer property to married couple or domestic partners "as community property with right of survivorship."
Shares of co-owners	May be unequal. (This is specified on the deed.)	All joint tenants must own equal shares.	Determined by partnership agreement or Uniform Partnership Act.	Each owns half.	Each owns half.
Survivorship	On co-owner's death, interest passes to heirs under intestate succession law or beneficiaries under will or living trust.	Deceased joint tenant's share automatically goes to surviving joint tenants.	Interests usually go to partner's heirs or beneficiaries, but partnership agreement may limit this.	Spouse or partner can leave his or her half to anyone; if nothing to the contrary, goes to surviving spouse or partner.	When one spouse or partner dies, survivor automatically owns entire property.
Probate	Interest left by will is subject to probate. Simplified procedure available if left to spouse.	No probate necessary to transfer title to surviving joint tenants.	Interest left by will is subject to probate.	Simplified probate procedure available to transfer title to survivor.	No probate necessary to transfer title to survivor.
Termination	Any co-owner may transfer his or her interest or get partition order from court. Co-owners can change the form of ownership by signing a new deed.	Joint tenant may transfer interest to himself or another as tenants in common, or may get partition order from court.	Governed by partnership agreement or Uniform Partnership Act.	Both spouses or partners must agree to transfers.	Both spouses or partners must agree.

To understand how the tax advantage for community property works, you need to know how federal capital gains tax is computed when a home is sold. Essentially, you are taxed on the difference between what you paid, plus the value of any capital improvements you've made, and what you sell the house for. (Capital improvements are those that increase the value of your property and have a useful life of more than a year—for example, new insulation or a new patio.) But you aren't taxed on the first $250,000 of capital gains ($500,000 for a couple) from the sale of a house, so this tax advantage now comes into play only when very large profits are made.

EXAMPLE: Carmen and Al buy a house for $100,000. Over the years they make $10,000 in capital improvements, and sell the place 25 years later for $650,000 (after costs of sale are subtracted). They have capital gains of $540,000, but they can exclude $500,000 of that amount from tax.

In tax lingo, the amount that Carmen and Al paid for the house ($100,000), plus the cost of improvements ($10,000), is their "tax basis" in the property ($110,000). The increase in the house's value over this basis, as reflected in the selling price, is taxable capital gain. So the higher the basis, the less capital gain when you sell.

Sale of Carmen and Al's house:

Sale Price	$650,000
Basis	− 110,000
Capital gain	$540,000

When a property owner dies, the new owner's tax basis in the inherited property automatically changes to the property's value at the former owner's death. If the value of the property has increased, the new owner's basis is called a "stepped-up" basis.

Let's go back to Carmen and Al and assume that they owned their house as joint tenants or tenants in common (not community property) and that Carmen died and left her half-interest in the property to Al. At Carmen's death, the basis for her half of the property would increase from $55,000 (half of the $100,000 purchase price and the $10,000 of improvements) to $325,000 (half of the value of the property at the time of her death). The basis in the other half of the property ($55,000) would remain the same. Al's total tax basis in the house would now be $380,000 ($325,000 plus $55,000). Now, when he sells the house for $650,000, he will have $270,000 in capital gains. The first $250,000 of that amount can be excluded from tax.

Sale after Carmen's death, if house had been held as separate (not community) property:

Sale Price	$650,000
Basis	− 380,000
Capital gain	$270,000

The advantage of community property is that the entire property, not just the half the surviving spouse inherits, gets a stepped-up tax basis. A survivor who wants to sell a house with a stepped-up basis soon after the first spouse dies will owe tax only on any increase in value since the first spouse's death. For example, if Al and Carmen had held their house as community property, both Al's and Carmen's shares (not just Carmen's) would receive a stepped-up basis when Carmen died. The new basis, at Carmen's death, would be $650,000—the value of the entire property at the time she died. If Al sold the property for $650,000 after Carmen's death, he would owe no federal capital gains tax on the transaction.

Sale after Carmen's death, if house had been held as community property:

Sale Price	$650,000
Basis	− 650,000
Capital gain	$ 0

Placing Property in Community Property With Right of Survivorship

It is easy to place property in community property form when the deed is drawn up from scratch. Simply write the deed, for example, "to Carmen Rivera and Albert Rivera, husband and wife, as community property with right of survivorship."

If you want to change your current property ownership arrangement to community property with right of survivorship, the best way is simply to execute a new deed to yourselves and record it in the county recorder's office.

> **EXAMPLE:** Carmen and Albert sign a new deed, transferring the property "from Carmen Rivera and Albert Rivera, as joint tenants, to Carmen Rivera and Albert Rivera, husband and wife, as community property with right of survivorship."

Be careful if one spouse gives up property rights. If you're thinking about turning one spouse's separate property into community property, you might want to see a lawyer first. If one spouse was unduly influenced by the other into making the change, a judge could invalidate it later.

Placing Property in Joint Tenancy or Tenancy in Common

Although holding title as community property with right of survivorship is usually preferable, in certain situations a married couple may prefer to put real estate in joint tenancy or tenancy in common. For example, a bank or savings and loan may insist, for purposes of its own, that the property be held in joint tenancy.

Before you take the property as joint tenants or tenants in common, you should read the discussion above about the features of these forms of ownership. If you want to convert property you own as community property, you should execute a new deed from yourselves "as community property" to yourselves "as joint tenants" or as "tenants in common."

Divorce. No matter how you hold title, California law will presume the property to be community property if you and your spouse or domestic partner split up. If you want to defeat this presumption, you can:

- state, on the deed, that the property is intended to be separate, not community property, and
- sign a separate agreement.

The deed and agreement would look like the ones shown below.

Consider seeing a lawyer—or two. In most circumstances, California law presumes that property owned by a married couple or registered domestic partners is community property. You can rebut that presumption by writing and signing an agreement stating that you don't want the property to be community property. But that can be tricky, too, because if one spouse gives up valuable property rights in the agreement, a court might later conclude that the spouse was unduly influenced by the other. The court could throw out the whole agreement. To be safe, you and your spouse should consult a lawyer—who may recommend that you each see separate lawyers.

Marital Property Agreement

Diane Holst and James Holst, husband and wife, agree as follows:

1. We purchased the apartment building at 9347 24th Street, Anaheim, California, with community property funds and Diane's separate property.

2. We hold title to the building as tenants in common.

3. Because of Diane's greater investment in the building and her efforts in managing it, she shall be entitled to 80% of the value of the building, and James shall be entitled to 20%, if our marriage ends in dissolution.

4. We intend this document to rebut the presumption of current Family Code § 2581 that property held in joint title is community property. We do not wish the property to be treated as community property for purposes of property division at dissolution.

Dated: _____   _____
                                                (signature)

Dated: _____   _____
                                                (signature)

State of California   )
)
County of _____)

On _____, before me, _____

_____, a notary public in and for said state, personally appeared

_____, personally known to me (or proved to me on the basis of satisfactory evidence) to be the person(s) whose name(s) is/are subscribed to the within instrument, and acknowledged to me that he/she/they executed the same in his/her/their authorized capacity(ies) and that by his/her/their signature(s) on the instrument the person(s), or the entity upon behalf of which the person(s) acted, executed the instrument.

_____
Signature of Notary

                                       [SEAL]

Recording requested by

Diane and James Holst
290 Gabriel Way
Albany, CA 94706

and when recorded mail
this deed and tax statements to

same as above

For recorder's use

Grant Deed

☑ This transfer is exempt from the documentary transfer tax.

☐ The documentary transfer tax is $_____ and is computed on:

    ☐ the full value of the interest or property conveyed.

    ☐ the full value less the value of liens or encumbrances remaining thereon at the time of sale.

The property is located in ☐ an unincorporated area. ☑ the city of ___Albany_____

For a valuable consideration, receipt of which is hereby acknowledged, ___Diane Holst and James Holst,___

as husband and wife,_____ hereby grant(s) to ___Diane Holst and James___

Holst, in joint tenancy, to be held as separate, not community property_____

the following real property in the City of ____Albany_____, County of ____Alameda_____ California:

Taking Title as Separate Property of One Spouse

If you're married but want to own real property separately, as an individual, you can take title in your name alone. Usually, this is appropriate only if the property is bought with money that belongs to one spouse separately. Broadly speaking, money is separate property if it was owned before marriage or acquired after permanent separation. In addition, gifts and inheritances received by one spouse are that spouse's separate property. If mortgage payments, taxes, or improvements are made to a house with community money (money earned or acquired by either spouse after marriage, except for gifts and inheritances) the house becomes at least partly community property, no matter what the deed says.

If title is to be put in the name of one married individual, it's best to execute and record an agreement declaring the couple's intent that the property be held as one spouse's separate property. Otherwise, if they divorce and disagree about ownership of the property, a court will characterize the property as community or separate according to what kind of funds (community or separate) paid for it, not whose name appears on the deed. Because it isn't always clear what type of property was used to pay for improvements, taxes, etc., the fight can be nasty.

A sample agreement is shown below.

Community Property Agreement

We, Brian Morgan and Laura Stein, husband and wife, hereby agree that:

1. Brian Morgan holds title to a vacation cabin near Lake Tahoe in California.

2. Although the cabin was purchased with savings that were community property, we intend it to be the separate property of Brian Morgan.

3. We make this agreement in light of the fact that Brian contributed more to purchase of the cabin than did Laura and that upon Brian's death, we both want the cabin to be inherited by Scott Morgan, Brian's son.

Dated: _____   _____
                                                  (signature)

Dated: _____   _____
                                                  (signature)

State of California   )
)

County of _____)

On _____, before me, _____

_____, a notary public in and for said state, personally appeared

_____, personally known to me (or proved to me on the basis of satisfactory evidence) to be the person(s) whose name(s) is/are subscribed to the within instrument, and acknowledged to me that he/she/they executed the same in his/her/their authorized capacity(ies) and that by his/her/their signature(s) on the instrument the person(s), or the entity upon behalf of which the person(s) acted, executed the instrument.

_____

Signature of Notary

                                                          [SEAL]

⚠ **Be careful if one spouse gives up property rights.** If one spouse or partner gives up valuable property rights in the agreement, a court might later conclude that the spouse was unduly influenced by the other. The court could throw out the whole agreement. To be safe, consult a lawyer—who may recommend that you each see separate lawyers.

Transfers to Partnerships

To transfer real estate to a partnership, the deed should be made out to the name the partnership does business under (the fictitious business name on file with the county or state), or to the partners by name. For example:

"to Elm Street Books, a partnership," or

"to Linda Stone and Blake Herbert, a partnership."

What the partners can do with the property once it is transferred to the partnership is governed either by the partnership agreement or, in the absence of an agreement, the Uniform Partnership Act. (Corp. Code §§ 16100 and following.)

 More on partnership property. See *Form a Partnership: The Complete Legal Guide*, by Denis Clifford and Ralph Warner (Nolo).

Transfers to Corporations

A corporation takes property in the corporation's name. You must specify the entity clearly so that there will be no confusion over who actually owns the property. If you don't, the transfer could be invalidated.

EXAMPLE: Jody wants to put property in the name of the flower shop she operates with her husband. The shop's name is "Jody and Don's Flower Shop." However, it was officially incorporated as "Jo-Don Flowers, Inc." The deed should be made out "to Jo-Don Flowers, Inc.," not to "Jody and Don's Flower Shop."

Transfers to Limited Liability Companies

A limited liability company (LLC) takes title to real estate in the name of the company. Just identify the company by name and state that it is a limited liability company organized under California law.

For example, a deed might be made out to "Deer Run Photographers, a California Limited Liability Company."

More on LLCs. *Your Limited Liability Company: An Operating Manual*, by Anthony Mancuso (Nolo), explains how LLC members should prepare and pass a formal resolution authorizing a real estate transfer.

Transfers to Minors

There is very seldom a good reason for giving real estate directly to a minor (someone less than 18 years old). In most cases, an adult will have to manage the property anyway, which means you must set up a trust or custodianship. We discuss these options below.

To a Custodian Under the Uniform Transfers to Minors Act

One way to give property to a minor is to transfer it to an adult as a "custodian" for the minor, under the California Uniform Transfers to Minors Act. (Prob. Code §§ 3900 and following.) This can be done either in a deed or in a will; most often, a will is used because there is rarely a good reason to want to transfer real property to a minor while you're alive and able to manage it yourself.

A property custodian's rights and duties are outlined by statute. A custodian must be prudent in management of the property and must keep certain records.

You may appoint only one person to manage property for a minor, but you can nominate alternate custodians to take over in case your first choice is unable or unwilling to serve. You must separately designate a custodian for each minor to whom you're giving property. A deed creating a custodianship would look like the one shown below.

The transfer becomes effective when the deed is recorded. It is irrevocable (you can't take it back). The custodian transfers the property to the minor outright when the minor turns 18, unless you specify a different age, up to 25 (see sample deed below).

To the Minor Directly

A minor can take title to real estate, but can't sell or mortgage it. An adult must manage the property on behalf of its young owner. You can, however, make a transfer directly to a minor by naming him in a deed like this: "to Scott Hawthorne, a minor."

Transfers to Living Trusts

A revocable living (inter vivos) trust is a probate avoidance device established by a living person, not in a will. The owner of property (the trustor, settlor, or grantor) transfers it to the trustee (who manages the property) and names a beneficiary. The trustee transfers ownership of the property to the beneficiary when the settlor dies. If the same property were left by will, it would probably have to go through probate, which takes months and can be costly.

Commonly, if you set up this kind of trust, you name yourself as trustee. This allows you to keep control over your property while you are alive and make sure it goes to the beneficiary, without probate, when you die. If you change your mind at

---

Recording requested by

Grace Henry
342 Grove Street
Mendocino, CA 93702

and when recorded mail
this deed and tax statements to

same as above

For recorder's use

Grant Deed

☑ This transfer is exempt from the documentary transfer tax.

☐ The documentary transfer tax is $_____ and is computed on:

    ☐ the full value of the interest or property conveyed.

    ☐ the full value less the value of liens or encumbrances remaining thereon at the time of sale.

The property is located in ☐ an unincorporated area. ☑ the city of ____Mendocino____

For a valuable consideration, receipt of which is hereby acknowledged, ____Sarah J. Hooper____

_____ hereby grant(s) to ____Grace Henry, as custodian____

____for David Campbell until age 21, under the California Uniform Transfers to Minors Act.____

the following real property in the City of ____Mendocino____, County of ____Mendocino____ California:

any time, you can simply revoke the trust or change the beneficiary.

The trust document names a successor trustee to take over when the original trustee dies. The successor trustee is directed to give the property to the beneficiary.

In most cases, because the trustee is none other than yourself, you simply transfer the property from yourself to yourself as trustee. Obviously, revoking the trust is a simple matter when you are the trustee; you merely transfer the property back to yourself.

To create a trust for real property, you must sign a trust document that appoints a trustee and sets out the terms of the trust—how the trustee is to manage the property, whether or not the trust is revocable, when ownership should be transferred to the beneficiary, and so on.

Creating a trust. For instructions on creating a living trust, see *Make Your Own Living Trust,* by Denis Clifford, or *Quicken WillMaker Plus* software (both from Nolo).

You'll need to prepare and sign a deed if you transfer real estate:

- to a trustee, or
- to a trust beneficiary when the time comes for the property to be distributed (see Chapter 2).

A sample is shown below.

Recording requested by

Marjorie Simmons
499 Sycamore Street
Anaheim, CA 98732

and when recorded mail
this deed and tax statements to

same as above

For recorder's use

Grant Deed

☑ This transfer is exempt from the documentary transfer tax.

☐ The documentary transfer tax is $_____ and is computed on:

   ☐ the full value of the interest or property conveyed.

   ☐ the full value less the value of liens or encumbrances remaining thereon at the time of sale.

The property is located in ☐ an unincorporated area. ☑ the city of ____Anaheim____

For a valuable consideration, receipt of which is hereby acknowledged, __Marjorie Simmons__

_____ hereby grant(s) to __Marjorie Simmons,__

____Trustee of the Marjorie Simmons Revocable Living Trust dated July 6, 20xx____

the following real property in the City of ____Anaheim____, County of ____Orange____ California:

You should record the deed with the county recorder in the county where the property is located (see Chapter 6).

If you're married or in a registered domestic partnership: As with any transfer from a married person, both you and your spouse or partner should sign the deed. Even if you are sure that the property you are putting in trust is your separate property, we recommend being on the safe side and having your spouse sign. (See Chapter 2.)

What's next: Once you have decided how the new owners of the property should take title, you're ready to go to Chapter 5 and prepare your deed. ■

Chapter 4

Deeds of Trust

A trust deed is not a conventional deed used to transfer ownership to real property; it is really the functional equivalent of a mortgage. Like a mortgage, a trust deed makes a piece of real property security for a loan to the property owner. If the loan is not repaid on time, the property can be sold (foreclosed on) by the lender and the proceeds used to pay it off. This chapter explains how trust deeds are used and how to fill one out.

Reminder: A trust deed is *not* used to transfer property to a living trust. The terminology is confusingly similar, but trust deeds and living trusts have almost nothing else in common. A living trust is a probate avoidance device; it is not used to provide security for a loan. Transfers to living trusts are discussed in Chapter 3.

Deeds of Trust: Cast of Characters

Trustor: The trustor is the borrower. The borrower owns the property but signs the trust deed giving the trustee power to sell it if he defaults on the loan.

Trustee: The trustee named in a trust deed does not exercise any control over the property; he has only the power to sell the property if the loan the trust deed secures is defaulted on. Frequently, a title insurance company serves as trustee.

Beneficiary: The lender is the beneficiary; if the property is sold, the lender is repaid from the proceeds.

How Trust Deeds Work

A trust deed is used in tandem with a promissory note that sets out the amount and terms of the loan. The borrower signs the note, which is a written promise to repay the borrowed money. A trust deed, which makes the property security for the loan, is also prepared. If the borrower defaults on the note, the trust deed allows the property to be sold (by the person named in the trust deed as the trustee) and the lender repaid from the proceeds. Any money left, after the lender is paid and the costs of sale are paid, goes to the borrower.

The trustee's power of sale. When the property owner executes a trust deed, he gives a third party, the "trustee," legal ownership of the property. The trustee is usually a title company or real estate broker. The trustee has no control over the property as long as the borrower makes the agreed-upon payments on the loan and fulfills the promises in the trust deed (for example, to take care of the property and keep up insurance). If the borrower defaults, however, the trustee has the power to sell the property, without having to file a court action, to pay off the loan.

EXAMPLE: Jan wants to borrow money from her brother Loren, using her house as security for the loan. He doesn't doubt that she'll pay him, but if for some reason she can't (because she dies, becomes incapacitated, or goes bankrupt), he wants to be assured of getting the property back without having to file a lawsuit. She signs a promissory note for the amount of the loan and a deed of trust that gives a trustee power to sell the house if she defaults on the loan. She is the trustor; Loren, who loaned her the money, is the beneficiary of the trust deed. As trustee, the trust deed names the ABC Title Company (how to pick a trustee is discussed below). The trustee has no powers unless Jan defaults on the loan and Loren wants to foreclose.

Reconveyance of title. When the loan is paid off, the trustee's and lender's interests end. The trustee executes and records a deed that reconveys title to the property back to the owner (the person who borrowed the money). (See "Reconveyance," below.)

Multiple deeds of trust. When a property owner borrows money from a family member, there is often already a deed of trust on the property—the one signed when an institutional lender financed the purchase of the property. That's no problem—an owner can keep signing trust deeds as long as lenders are willing to lend money on the property. A lender won't be willing to accept a trust deed as security for a loan when it appears that, if the property is foreclosed on and sold, the proceeds of sale won't be enough to pay off its loan.

> **EXAMPLE:** Suzanne asks Adam for a loan of $25,000, offering her house as security. The house, which is worth $250,000, already has a $200,000 deed of trust on it. Adam says no. He knows that if the house were sold at a foreclosure sale it might well bring less than it's really worth, and that by the time the first trust deed holder and the costs of sale were paid off, he wouldn't get his money back.

If the property is sold and there's not enough money to pay off all the encumbrances on the property (deeds of trust and liens), liens are paid off in the order they were recorded. Thus the holder of a second trust deed (often just called a "second") only gets what's left after the first trust deed is paid off. State statutes, however, contain a fairly complicated system of preferences and priorities. Property tax liens, for example, must always be paid off first.

> **EXAMPLE:** Stephen defaults on a loan from Rebecca secured by a deed of trust on his property. He is also behind in his property tax payments, and the county has recorded a tax lien on the property. If Rebecca forecloses on the property and has the property sold, the tax lien will be paid first, and what's left over will be applied to the debt secured by the deed of trust.

How to Fill Out a Trust Deed and Promissory Note

As explained above, a trust deed makes real estate security for a loan. So if you have a trust deed, you will also need to prepare a promissory note that provides written evidence of the underlying debt. We explain how to draw up both the deed and the note.

Basically, a trust deed must identify the parties to the transaction and the property being given as security. It also must contain a statement that the deed of trust secures the obligation to repay a certain amount to the beneficiary. And, like other deeds, the signed original should be notarized, recorded, and delivered to the beneficiary. Because parts of a trust deed look a lot like a grant deed, these instructions occasionally refer you to Chapter 5, which contains instructions for filling out grant and quitclaim deeds.

The Deed of Trust

Here are instructions for filling out the deed of trust included in the appendix of this book. The deed of trust is a standard one, used by Freddie Mac. These instructions follow the headings on the form.

Trust deeds are exempt from the documentary transfer tax, so the deed form doesn't include tax information. (Rev. and Tax. Code § 11921.)

After Recording Return To

The lender will want to receive the original trust deed, so the lender's name goes in the top space.

(A) "Security Instrument"

Here, fill in the date the trust deed is signed.

(B) "Borrower"

The name and address of the person borrowing the money and giving his property as security go in this blank. The names of all owners of the property, and their spouses, must be included to give the entire property (all owners' interests in the property) as security. A co-owner can only give as security his interest in the property. In other words, a lender wants to be sure that all owners and their spouses sign the deed of trust as a condition of lending the money (unless the lender is willing to take as security one co-owner's interest in property). The rules for who must sign a deed of trust are the same as for other deeds. See Chapter 2.

(C) "Lender"

Here, fill in the name and address of the person who lent the borrower money. If the lender is a business, fill in the second sentence as well—for example, "Lender is a corporation organized and existing under the laws of California." If the lender is not a business entity, you can cross out that sentence.

(D) "Trustee"

In the most common kind of real estate transactions, where a bank or savings and loan finances the purchase of real estate, the trustee is almost always a title or trust company. Sometimes real estate brokers act as trustees.

Attorneys commonly write in the name of a title company as trustee on a trust deed, without consulting the title company. Title companies even give out trust deed forms with their names already printed in the "trustee" space. They don't mind being named as trustee because a trustee has nothing to do unless the borrower defaults. If the borrower pays off the loan without defaulting (as happens in most cases), the title company then executes and records a deed reconveying the property to the borrower.

If the borrower does default, the trustee has the power to sell the property to pay off the loan. Most title or escrow companies turn the deed over to a professional foreclosure firm.

(E) "Note"

This statement identifies the promissory note that was executed to evidence the underlying debt (a tear-out note is in the appendix). You should fill in the date the note was signed and the amount of the debt. Also enter the date by which the note will be repaid.

(F) "Property"

The trust deed must adequately describe the property that is being given as security. On page 2 of the form, you'll fill in the street address.

(G) "Loan"

You don't need to fill anything in here.

(H) "Riders"

You shouldn't need to check any of these boxes. They are used only if any additional agreements—for example, about a large "balloon" payment—are attached to the deed of trust.

TRANSFER OF RIGHTS IN THE PROPERTY

In the first blank, fill in "county." In the second blank, fill in the name of the county where the property is located. In the remaining blanks, fill in the street address of the property.

Now you can skip to the last page of the form. Everything in the middle is standard language about the rights of the lender and borrower. For example, the borrower promises to keep the property in good repair, pay real estate taxes, and otherwise protect the lender's investment. If the borrower breaks one of these promises, the trustee can foreclose on the property. The trustee's powers are also set out.

Signatures

Here, the trustors (borrowers) sign the deed. All named trustors must sign.

Acknowledgment (Notarization)

A notary public fills in this section. See Chapter 5 for instructions on how to get your deed notarized.

The Promissory Note

The following promissory note is taken from *101 Law Forms for Personal Use,* by Robin Leonard and Ralph Warner (Nolo), which explains in greater detail the choices you have when drawing up a promissory note. This note allows for installment payments of the debt and includes interest. You can remove those provisions if you want the loan repaid all at once, in a lump sum, or if you don't want to charge interest. A tear-out copy of the note is included in the appendix.

⚠ **This form isn't for businesses.** Like the other forms in this book, this promissory note should not be used in a commercial context. Special state and federal laws apply to notes used by businesses lending money to collect interest.

After Recording Return To:

Helen D. Whiteclyffe

73 Bloomsbury Road

Mount Hamilton, CA 93766

_____[Space Above This Line For Recording Data]_____

DEED OF TRUST

DEFINITIONS

Words used in multiple sections of this document are defined below and other words are defined in Sections 3, 11, 13, 18, 20 and 21. Certain rules regarding the usage of words used in this document are also provided in Section 16.

(A) **"Security Instrument"** means this document, which is dated __March 27, 20xx__ , _____, together with all Riders to this document.

(B) "Borrower" is __James Chadwick, 8800 Primrose Place, Niles, CA 93767__ . Borrower is the trustor under this Security Instrument.

(C) **"Lender"** is __Helen D Whiteclyffe__ . ~~Lender is a~~ _____ ~~organized and existing under the laws of~~ _____ . Lender's address is __73 Bloomsbury Road.__ __Mount Hamilton, CA 93766__ . Lender is the beneficiary under this Security Instrument.

(D) **"Trustee"** is __XYZ Title Company__ .

(E) **"Note"** means the promissory note signed by Borrower and dated __March 26, 20xx__ , _____. The Note states that Borrower owes Lender __fifty thousand__ _____ Dollars (U.S. $__50,000.00__) plus interest. Borrower has promised to pay this debt in regular Periodic Payments and to pay the debt in full not later than __April 1, 20xx__ .

(F) **"Property"** means the property that is described below under the heading "Transfer of Rights in the Property."

(G) **"Loan"** means the debt evidenced by the Note, plus interest, any prepayment charges and late charges due under the Note, and all sums due under this Security Instrument, plus interest.

(H) **"Riders"** means all Riders to this Security Instrument that are executed by Borrower. The following Riders are to be executed by Borrower [check box as applicable]:

☐ Adjustable Rate Rider   ☐ Condominium Rider   ☐ Second Home Rider
☐ Balloon Rider   ☐ Planned Unit Development Rider   ☐ Other(s) [specify] _____
☐ 1-4 Family Rider   ☐ Biweekly Payment Rider

CALIFORNIA--Single Family--Fannie Mae/Freddie Mac **UNIFORM INSTRUMENT**   Form 3005   1/01   *(page 1 of 16 pages)*

Identification of parties. First, check the appropriate box, depending on how many people are signing the note. Remember that because of community property rules, spouses and registered domestic partners must sign notes secured by a deed of trust even if title to the property is in only one spouse's name. (See Chapter 2.) Then fill in the name and address of the lender and the amount the borrower is to pay back.

Interest rates. Typical interest rates for family and personal debts range widely. In general, anything higher than 10% for personal and family loans violates the California usury (excessive interest) laws. Although loans for the purchase of real estate may be exempt from the 10% limit, the law in this area is terminally confusing. Stick to the 10% ceiling unless you check with a lawyer.

Be careful with low interest, too. If you charge significantly less than the market rate, you should be aware that the IRS may treat the money the borrower is saving (compared to borrowing at the going rate of interest) as a gift. This is a problem only when the amount of money loaned is huge and the total gift exceeds the annual federal gift tax exemption, which is currently $12,000 (see Chapter 1).

Prepayment provisions. The first option does not allow credit for prepayment; the borrower must pay interest at the indicated rate for the entire loan period (and beyond if repayment is delayed). The second choice allows the loan to be prepaid, and interest is therefore charged only for the length of the time the loan is actually outstanding.

Amount of installment payments. Fill in the amount of the borrower's monthly payments. If no interest is being charged, figuring the amount of the payments is easy: just divide the amount of the loan by the number of months until it is due. If interest is being charged, consult the amortization schedule below. First, find the figure where the row with your interest rate and the column with the period of your loan intersect. To calculate the amount of the monthly payment, multiply that figure by the total amount of the loan.

Amortization Schedule

Interest Rate	1	1.5	2	2.5	3	4	5	6	7	8	9	10
4.0%	0.0851	0.0573	0.0434	0.0351	0.0295	0.0226	0.0184	0.0156	0.0137	0.0122	0.0110	0.0101
4.5%	0.0854	0.0576	0.0436	0.0353	0.0297	0.0228	0.0186	0.0159	0.0139	0.0124	0.0113	0.0104
5.0%	0.0856	0.0578	0.0439	0.0355	0.0300	0.0230	0.0189	0.0161	0.0141	0.0127	0.0115	0.0106
5.5%	0.0858	0.0580	0.0441	0.0358	0.0302	0.0233	0.0191	0.0163	0.0144	0.0129	0.0118	0.0109
6.0%	0.0861	0.0582	0.0443	0.0360	0.0304	0.0235	0.0193	0.0166	0.0146	0.0131	0.0120	0.0111
6.5%	0.0863	0.0585	0.0445	0.0362	0.0306	0.0237	0.0196	0.0168	0.0148	0.0134	0.0123	0.0114
7.0%	0.0865	0.0587	0.0448	0.0364	0.0309	0.0239	0.0198	0.0170	0.0151	0.0136	0.0125	0.0116
7.5%	0.0868	0.0589	0.0450	0.0367	0.0311	0.0242	0.0200	0.0173	0.0153	0.0139	0.0128	0.0119
8.0%	0.0870	0.0591	0.0452	0.0369	0.0313	0.0244	0.0203	0.0175	0.0156	0.0141	0.0130	0.0121
8.5%	0.0872	0.0594	0.0455	0.0371	0.0316	0.0246	0.0205	0.0178	0.0158	0.0144	0.0133	0.0124
9.0%	0.0875	0.0596	0.0457	0.0373	0.0318	0.0249	0.0208	0.0180	0.0161	0.0147	0.0135	0.0127
9.5%	0.0877	0.0598	0.0459	0.0376	0.0320	0.0251	0.0210	0.0183	0.0163	0.0149	0.0138	0.0129
10.0%	0.0879	0.0601	0.0461	0.0378	0.0323	0.0254	0.0212	0.0185	0.0166	0.0152	0.0141	0.0132

Promissory Note Secured by Deed of Trust

1. For value received,   ☐ I individually   ☐ We jointly and severally   promise to pay to the order of
_____ [*person(s) to whom debt is owed*]_____

$_____ at _____ [*address where payment is to be made*]_____

_____ with interest at the rate of _____% per year: [*choose one*]

   ☐ from the date this note is signed until the date it is due or is paid in full, whichever date occurs last.

   ☐ from the date this note is signed until the date it is paid in full.

2. The signer(s) of this note also agree that this note shall be paid in installments, which include principal and interest, of not less than $_____ per month, due on the first day of each month, until such time as the principal and interest are paid in full.

3. If any installment payment due under this note is not received by the holder within _____ days of its due date, the entire amount of unpaid principal shall become immediately due and payable at the option of the holder without prior notice to the signer(s) of this note.

4. If the holder(s) of this note prevail(s) in a lawsuit to collect on it, the signer(s) agree(s) to pay the holder(s)' attorney fees in an amount the court finds to be just and reasonable.

5. Signer(s) agree(s) that until such time as the principal and interest owed under this note are paid in full, the note shall be secured by a deed of trust to real property commonly known as _[*address or other*____

   description]_____, owned by _[*name*]_____

   _____ executed on _____ [*date signed*]_____ at

   _[*place signed*]_____ and recorded on

   _[*date recorded*]_____ in the records of _____ County, California.

_____   _____
Date   Date

_____   _____
Location (city or county)   Location (city or county)

_____   _____
Address   Address

_____   _____

_____   _____

_____   _____
Signature of Borrower   Signature of Borrower

State of California

County of _____ }

On _____, before me, _____,

a notary public in and for said state, personally appeared _____

personally known to me (or proved to me on the basis of satisfactory evidence) to be the person(s) whose name(s) is/are subscribed to the within instrument, and acknowledged to me that he/she/they executed the same in his/her/their authorized capacity(ies) and that by his/her/their signature(s) on the instrument the person(s), or entity upon behalf of which the person(s) acted, executed the instrument.

                                                              [SEAL]

_____
Signature of Notary

EXAMPLE: If your interest rate is 10% and the loan will be outstanding for five years, the figure from the amortization chart is 0.0212. Assuming a loan amount of $10,000, the monthly payments will each be .0212 x $10,000, or $212.

Acceleration clause. This paragraph is a standard, though harsh-sounding, clause that allows the lender to declare the entire loan due if the borrower misses one payment by a certain number of days (five, 15, 30—whatever you want). That way, the lender can ask for the whole debt in one lawsuit. Otherwise, she would have to either bring a new suit every time a payment was missed (for the amount of that payment), or wait until all the installments should have been paid and then sue for the whole amount. Obviously, either of those options is impractical—hence the need for the acceleration clause.

Attorney's fees. This provision makes the loser in a lawsuit responsible for the other side's attorney fees. Unless this clause is included, a small or medium-sized note is virtually uncollectible, because it costs more to collect it than it's worth. If for any reason you don't want to include this clause, just cross it out and have the borrower initial it.

Reference to deed of trust. Just as the deed of trust refers to the promissory note, the note refers to the deed of trust. Fill in the address of the property, the owners' names, and the dates and places the deed was signed and recorded.

Date and signature. Here, the borrower (property owner) signs and dates the note.

Notarization. Unlike a deed, the signatures on a promissory note do not have to be notarized. However, since you've got to have the trust deed notarized anyway, it's not a bad idea to go ahead and pay the nominal cost of having the note notarized too.

Delivery of the deed. After the trust deed and promissory note have been signed, you are ready to deliver the original deed to the beneficiary. Chapter 5 explains delivery. The borrower (trustor) should get a copy of the deed and note.

Checklist for Preparing a Trust Deed and Promissory Note

Does the trust deed:

☐ identify the trustor (borrower/property owner)

☐ identify the trustee (third party who will handle foreclosure if necessary)

☐ identify the beneficiary (lender for whom the property is security)

☐ describe the property accurately and completely, and

☐ refer to the promissory note evidencing the underlying debt?

Was the deed:

☐ signed by the trustor(s) (all owners of the property giving their interests as security, and their spouses)

☐ dated

☐ notarized, and

☐ "delivered" to the beneficiary?

Does the promissory note:

☐ identify the lender and borrower

☐ set out the terms of the loan: interest rate, monthly payments, length of the loan period, and

☐ refer to the deed of trust?

Was the note:

☐ signed and dated by the borrower (and spouse), and

☐ notarized?

The next step: After you've prepared the trust deed and promissory note, go to Chapter 6 for instructions on how to record the trust deed.

Reconveyance

When a promissory note is paid off, title to the property is reconveyed to the borrower, so that the borrower owns the property free and clear. The trustee—that is, whatever title company you filled in the "trustee" blank when you prepared the original deed of trust—must sign the deed that reconveys title to the borrower.

The trustee, however, will do nothing until instructed by the lender. So a borrower who wants to get a reconveyance started should get together with the lender and take several documents to the trustee:

- the original promissory note
- the original deed of trust, and
- a reconveyance deed (sometimes this is printed on the back of the original deed of trust; if not, a grant deed is fine).

The trustee will have the lender sign a "Request for Full Reconveyance" form. Then the trustee will sign and record a deed that transfers (reconveys) title from the trustee to the borrower.

> **EXAMPLE:** Jason borrowed $10,000 from his parents to finance the remodeling of his home. When he borrowed the money, he signed a deed of trust, giving the house as security. He named his parents as beneficiaries and a local title company as trustee.
>
> After five years, when Jason has paid off the loan, he goes to the title company and gets a Request for Full Reconveyance form. His parents sign it, authorizing the trustee (the title company) to reconvey the property to Jason. After the title company prepares and records the deed, Jason's parents no longer have a security interest in the property.

∎

Preparing Your Deed

A deed is the document, signed by the person transferring real property, that actually transfers title to the property from one person (or business entity) to another. The essential parts of all deeds are:

- identification of the grantor (person making the transfer)
- identification of the grantee (person receiving the deed)
- words transferring the property
- a description of the property being transferred, and
- signature of the grantor.

Notarization isn't necessary for the validity of a deed, but it is required before you can record the deed with the county recorder.

Why isn't an oral agreement to transfer property enough? The short answer is because the law says it isn't. The idea behind the requirement of a formal, signed deed is to prevent confusion about who owns land. The goal of the whole system is to have a reliable and easily accessible written record of every transaction involving land. The crucial elements of the system are:

- a written deed, executed with enough detail and formality to make it reliable, and
- a recording system that keeps in one place, as public records, all deeds for land in a particular county (recording is discussed in Chapter 6).

"With This Clod ..."

Under early English common law, no documents were needed to transfer land, and no records were kept of transfers. In a society where most people stayed put, and most real property passed from father to eldest son, there was little need for either. To transfer land, the owner made the symbolic gesture of going to the property and handing the new owner a clod of dirt, a stone, or a stick. The little ceremony, done in front of witnesses, was called "livery of seisin"—feudal legalese for "delivery of title."

A deed is usually a simple one-page document. It's easy to prepare by filling in the blanks on the tear-out forms in this book. There are a few formalities, however, that must be followed to make a deed legally valid and fully effective. If you're the owner (grantor), you must have your signature on the deed notarized and "deliver" the deed to the new owner (grantee). The grantee should promptly record the deed with the county recorder. The formalities surrounding deeds are another vestige of the tremendous importance English society placed on land transactions. Courts still take them quite seriously, however, and you should, too.

What Kind of Deed to Use

So now you're ready to do what you set out to do—draw up a deed. How do you start? The first step is to choose, based on what you're trying to accomplish, among the different deed forms used in California. It's usually a very easy choice to make.

Three different kinds of deeds are used to transfer land in California: grant, quitclaim, and warranty deeds. (If, instead of transferring the land, you want to give it as security for a debt, go to Chapter 4, which covers deeds of trust.) Tear-out copies of grant and quitclaim deeds are in the appendix. Let's look at each type in detail.

Grant Deeds

If you're transferring property outright, creating or changing ownership of co-owned property, or transferring property to or from a trustee, you probably need a grant deed.

A grant deed is the most commonly used kind of deed in California. It does the job for most transfers, especially intrafamily transfers. For example, a grant deed is appropriate if you want to:

- transfer property you own yourself to someone else
- transfer your interest as a co-owner to another co-owner

Transfer to Married Couple

Recording requested by

WALTER SINCLAIR and EVE SINCLAIR
8714 Hayes Street
Pasadena, California 92480

and when recorded mail
this deed and tax statements to

same as above

For recorder's use

Grant Deed

☑ This transfer is exempt from the documentary transfer tax.

☐ The documentary transfer tax is $_____ and is computed on:

    ☐ the full value of the interest or property conveyed.

    ☐ the full value less the value of liens or encumbrances remaining thereon at the time of sale.

The property is located in ☐ an unincorporated area. ☑ the city of _____Pasadena_____

For a valuable consideration, receipt of which is hereby acknowledged, ALEXANDER SINCLAIR and EMMA SINCLAIR, husband and wife, _____ hereby grant(s) to WALTER SINCLAIR AND EVE SINCLAIR, husband and wife, as community property

the following real property in the City of _____Pasadena_____, County of _____Los Angeles_____ California:

Portion of Lots 14 and 15, Block 3, of the Del Mar Tract, filed March 21, 1934, Map Book B, page 187, Los Angeles County records, described as follows: Beginning on the east line of Powell Street, distant thereon north 0°45' west 59 feet from southwest corner of Block 3; thence from the point of beginning north 0°45' east along Powell Street 60 feet; thence southeast along the south line of Clay Street 113 feet to the point of beginning.

Date: July 19, 20xx   *Emma Sinclair*

Date: July 19, 20xx   *Alexander Sinclair*

Date: _____   _____

Date: _____   _____

State of California

County of _____Los Angeles_____

On _____July 19, 20xx_____, before me, Kimberly Johnson,

a notary public in and for said state, personally appeared Emma Sinclair and Alexander Sinclair,

personally known to me (or proved to me on the basis of satisfactory evidence) to be the person(s) whose name(s) is/are subscribed to the within instrument, and acknowledged to me that he/she/they executed the same in his/her/their authorized capacity(ies) and that by his/her/their signature(s) on the instrument the person(s), or entity upon behalf of which the person(s) acted, executed the instrument.

Kimberly Johnson   [SEAL]
Signature of Notary

- transfer property from a married couple to someone else
- change the way co-owners hold title to property, for example, from joint tenancy to community property or tenancy in common
- transfer property to or from a trust, or
- transfer property to a custodian for a minor, under the Uniform Transfers to Minors Act.

Instructions for filling out a grant deed are below.

After-Acquired Title

If for some reason someone who executes a grant deed does not actually have title to the property, the grantee gets nothing, because the grantor had nothing to give. But if the grantor later acquires title, that "after-acquired title" automatically passes to the grantee. (Civ. Code § 1106.)

EXAMPLE: Ed buys a house from Lorrie. Under the impression that Lorrie has signed a deed and sent it to him, Ed decides to put title jointly in his name and that of his wife. He executes and records a grant deed conveying the property to himself and his wife. Lorrie, however, changes her mind and doesn't sign or send the deed. The deed to Ed and his wife transfers nothing because Ed didn't own the property.

Later, Lorrie changes her mind again and sends Ed the deed. Under the rule of after-acquired title, Ed's wife also now owns a half-interest in the property.

This rule is not as arcane as it may seem. In times of ferment in the real estate market, investors and agencies often buy and sell many pieces of property in a short period of time. When the timing of the deals means that property is sold before the seller has clear title, the doctrine of after-acquired title helps clean up the mess.

Quitclaim Deeds

If you just want to release a possible claim to land—if, for example, you want to release a possible community property interest in property, clearing the way for your spouse or ex-spouse to sell or mortgage it—then use a quitclaim deed.

A quitclaim deed makes no promises whatsoever about the property interest being conveyed. Essentially, it means that the person who signs the deed is conveying whatever interest—if any—she has in the property. If the person does own the property, or an interest in it, the quitclaim deed is as effective to transfer ownership of that interest as a grant deed. If she doesn't own an interest in the property, the recipient gets nothing.

As you might expect, a quitclaim deed is most useful when ownership of some parcel (or part of the parcel) of property is uncertain. It is commonly used when some person has a potential claim (often, a community property claim) to a piece of property that another person wants to sell. To avoid conflicts later, the person with the potential claim executes a quitclaim deed relinquishing all rights in the property.

If you are married and want to transfer property without your spouse's signature on the deed (or if you're divorcing and think you'll want to sell the property later), your spouse should execute a quitclaim deed giving her interest to you, even if you think your separate ownership of the property is perfectly clear. A bank or title company will insist on it. And even if a financial institution isn't involved in the current transaction, one is sure to be in on the act sometime in the future. Then, when the bank has the title checked and finds the transfer from only one spouse, it will undoubtedly insist on a quitclaim deed from the other spouse. It's easier to do it now than later. (See Chapter 2.)

EXAMPLE: Sue and Peter are getting divorced. They agree that Sue should keep the house. To ensure that Sue can prove, if she wants to sell or borrow against the house later, that it is really her separate property, Peter executes

Recording requested by
SUSAN E. DURANT
8729 Marin
Berkeley, CA 94707

and when recorded mail
this deed and tax statements to

same as above

For recorder's use

Quitclaim Deed

☑ This transfer is exempt from the documentary transfer tax.

☐ The documentary transfer tax is $_____ and is computed on:

    ☐ the full value of the interest or property conveyed.

    ☐ the full value less the value of liens or encumbrances remaining thereon at the time of sale.

The property is located in ☐ an unincorporated area. ☑ the city of _Berkeley_____

For a valuable consideration, receipt of which is hereby acknowledged, _Peter S. Durant_____

_____ hereby quitclaim(s) to ___Susan E. Durant____

_____

the following real property in the City of ____Berkeley_____, County of __Alameda_____California:

Lot 7 of the Vernon Park Tract, filed May 17, 1964, in Book 48 of Maps, at page 132, in the Office of the County Recorder of Alameda County, Oakland, California

Date: _February 3, 20xx_____   _Peter S. Durant_____

Date: _____   _____

Date: _____   _____

Date: _____   _____

State of California

County of ___Alameda_____ }

On _February 3, 20xx_____, before me, ___Mamie White_____,

a notary public in and for said state, personally appeared _Peter S. Durant_____,

personally known to me (or proved to me on the basis of satisfactory evidence) to be the person(s) whose name(s) is/are subscribed to the within instrument, and acknowledged to me that he/she/they executed the same in his/her/their authorized capacity(ies) and that by his/her/their signature(s) on the instrument the person(s), or entity upon behalf of which the person(s) acted, executed the instrument.

_Mamie White_____   [SEAL]
Signature of Notary

and records a quitclaim deed, giving to Sue any interest he might have in the house. When that's done, the public record will show title insurance companies, financial institutions, and potential buyers that Peter has no community property interest in the house.

Quitclaim deeds can also be used to settle uncertainty or disputes about other kinds of claims, including easements or rights to inherited property.

EXAMPLE 1: Andy wants to sell his house to Bill, but Bill is reluctant to buy because Andy's next-door neighbor, Marsha, has an easement that lets her use Andy's driveway to get to the back of her property. Andy explains the situation to Marsha, who is willing to give up the easement, which she seldom uses, for a payment of a few hundred dollars. She signs a quitclaim deed giving to Andy all rights (including the easement) she has in Andy's property, which means Bill can take the property free of her rights.

EXAMPLE 2: Nathan's will was written ambiguously, so that it wasn't clear which of his daughters, or both, should inherit his house. The daughters, Lauren and Jane, settled the matter themselves, agreeing that Lauren should have the house and Jane should take some other property. As part of the settlement, Jane executes a quitclaim deed to Lauren, giving up any right she may have to the house.

After-acquired title note: The doctrine of after-acquired title (see above) does not apply to quitclaim deeds, because someone who executes a quitclaim deed expressly transfers only whatever interest he has at the time. Thus if you receive a quitclaim deed from a person who doesn't actually have any interest in the property, and that person later does acquire some interest, you will not own that interest (unless a court finds some other doctrine that justifies giving it to you).

EXAMPLE: Michael executes a quitclaim deed to Sally. Sally records it and then discovers that Michael didn't have title to the land when he signed the deed, but got it the next day. Sally owns nothing; Michael still owns the property. He gave her (in the quitclaim deed) only the interest he had at that time, which was nothing.

Instructions for filling out a quitclaim deed are below.

Warranty Deeds

A warranty deed, by which the grantor guarantees that he has good title to the property, is appropriate only when you want to custom-design your deed to take care of certain specialized problems with the transaction. This book doesn't include a warranty deed.

A warranty deed contains express (not implied, as in the grant deed) promises about the title being transferred. Warranty deeds are seldom used at all these days; their function has largely been taken over by title insurance, which guarantees that the grantor has good title to the property (see Chapter 1). About the only situation left where a warranty deed is useful is a commercial transaction, where the parties want to add their own special provisions and promises (termed "covenants") to the deed.

Preparing a Grant or Quitclaim Deed

Finally! You're ready to fill out your deed. You've done the hard part of the transfer procedure already by making all the decisions about how to take title and who should sign. All that's left is the mechanical process of filling in the blanks.

Tear-out blank grant and quitclaim deeds are included in the appendix of this book.

Language note: California statutes (Gov't. Code § 27293) require a deed to be written in English unless an English translation, certified accurate by a court, is attached.

Deed Language, Or Is This English?

Printed deed forms (the kind you get from office supply stores) are given varying names. The most common titles are "Grant Deed" and "Quitclaim Deed." Others are headed "Joint Tenancy Deed." The important thing to know is that no matter what the title you have a grant deed, legally, any time the word "grant" is used in the deed itself. For example, a document that contains this language is a grant deed: "Jane Vanelli hereby grants to John Goodwin the following described property ...." Obviously, however, you shouldn't use a printed "Joint Tenancy Deed" unless you want to create a joint tenancy, simply because otherwise it's confusing.

The phrasing of form deeds also tends to be ridiculously formal and antiquated. It's still not uncommon to find grant deeds peppered with bold Gothic text proclaiming that the signer "grants, gives, bargains, sells, aliens, releases, enfeoffs, conveys, and confirms" his property to the new owner "to have and to hold." By the time you've read it all, you're not sure whether you're selling property or getting married. This excess language is at best unnecessary and at worst confusing. Our forms avoid it; if you're stuck with someone else's form, you can ignore it.

The following instructions are keyed to the sample deed shown below. Preparing the deed isn't difficult, but pay attention to the details. It's worth taking a little time to do it right.

1 Enter Recording Information

The new owner has the responsibility for recording a deed with the county recorder, so his or her name goes in the "Recording Requested By" space. (Chapter 6 explains recording.)

2 Enter Address for Tax Statements

Property tax statements should be mailed to the new owner, so enter his name and address here. If there is more than one new owner, one name and address is sufficient. Be sure to fill this in; it is required by statute. (Gov't. Code § 27321.5.) Some counties also require the tax roll parcel number of the property to be put on the deed. Find out by calling your county assessor or recorder. You can get the parcel number from an old property tax statement. Just type it in the margin of the deed. ("A.P.N." stands for "assessor's parcel number.")

3 Enter Documentary Transfer Tax Information

The deed should state whether or not the transfer is subject to a local documentary transfer tax, which is levied when real property is sold and the deed is recorded (see Chapter 1). (Rev. & Tax. Code § 11911.)

Gifts of real property and transfers between spouses or registered domestic partners dividing marital property are exempt from the tax. If your transfer is exempt from the tax, you should check the box in front of "This transfer is exempt from the documentary transfer tax" and attach a short signed statement that explicitly says why the transfer is exempt.

Gifts. A statement you can use if the transfer is a gift is shown below. (Property held in a revocable living trust is exempt from documentary transfer tax because it is a gift. It is not a gift for federal gift tax purposes, however, because the transfer is revocable at any time.) A tear-out copy is in the appendix.

Marital property division. To show why your transfer is exempt from the tax, one spouse (either one) should sign a declaration that states the transfer is made to divide community property between spouses in contemplation of divorce. This exemption does not apply to all transfers between spouses. Only if a court has issued a judgment or order dividing the property or the spouses, in contemplation of divorce, have signed a written agreement about

Recording requested by

(1)

and when recorded mail
this deed and tax statements to

(2)

For recorder's use

Grant Deed

(3) ☐ This transfer is exempt from the documentary transfer tax.

☐ The documentary transfer tax is $_____ and is computed on:

  ☐ the full value of the interest or property conveyed.

  ☐ the full value less the value of liens or encumbrances remaining thereon at the time of sale.

The property is located in ☐ an unincorporated area. ☐ the city of _____

For a valuable consideration, receipt of which is hereby acknowledged, **(4)** _____

_____ **(5)** hereby grant(s) to **(6)** _____

_____

the following real property in the City of _____, County of _____ California:

(7)

(8)

(9)

Date: _____ **(10)** _____

Date: _____ _____

Date: _____ _____

Date: _____ _____

State of California

County of _____ }

On _____, before me, _____,

a notary public in and for said state, personally appeared **(11)** _____,

personally known to me (or proved to me on the basis of satisfactory evidence) to be the person(s) whose name(s) is/are subscribed to the within instrument, and acknowledged to me that he/she/they executed the same in his/her/their authorized capacity(ies) and that by his/her/their signature(s) on the instrument the person(s), or entity upon behalf of which the person(s) acted, executed the instrument.

_____ [SEAL]
Signature of Notary

Declaration of Exemption From Documentary Transfer Tax: Gift of Real Property

Grantor has not received and will not receive consideration from grantee for the transfer made by the attached deed. Therefore, under Revenue and Taxation Code Sec. 11911, the transfer is not subject to the Documentary Transfer Tax.

I declare under penalty of perjury under the laws of California that the foregoing is true and correct.

_____

Grantor

Date: _____   _____, California

_____

Grantor

Date: _____   _____, California

---

how to divide property, is the transfer exempt. The appropriate reason should be checked on the declaration shown below. A sample declaration is shown below; a tear-out copy is in the appendix.

If the transfer is subject to the tax, fill in the amount of the tax on the deed. You can find out the amount by calling the county recorder before you take in or mail the deed to record it. You must pay the tax (to the county recorder) before you can record the deed.

Counties are allowed to levy a documentary transfer tax of up to 55¢ per $500 (or part thereof) of the sale price (less the amount of any liens on the property, including deeds of trust, taken over by the new owner) when real property is sold. Some cities add taxes, so the actual rate may be much higher.

The tax is figured on the value of the property transferred minus any liens remaining on it, so check the second box under the line with the amount unless there are no liens or encumbrances on the property.

EXAMPLE: Hannah sells some property to her son, Nathan. The property is subject to a deed of trust and a tax lien. Hannah pays the tax lien before the transfer and Nathan takes responsibility for (assumes) the deed of trust. The documentary transfer tax will be figured on the value of the property minus the amount of the trust deed. On the deed, Hannah should check:

☐ the full value less the value of liens or encumbrances …

If Nathan were not taking the property subject to any liens or encumbrances, Hannah would check:

☐ the full value of the interest or property conveyed.

④ Identify Grantor

Here is where you fill in the names of all current owners of the property—the persons who will sign the deed.

Declaration of Exemption From Documentary Transfer Tax: Division of Marital Real Property

The transfer made by the attached deed is made for the purpose of dividing community, quasi-community or quasi-marital real property between spouses, as required by:

☐ a judgment decreeing a dissolution of the marriage or legal separation, by a judgment of nullity, or by any other judgment or order rendered pursuant to Part 5 of Division 4 of the Civil Code, or

☐ a written agreement between the spouses executed in contemplation of such a judgment or order.

Therefore, under Revenue and Taxation Code Sec. 11927, the deed is not subject to the Documentary Transfer Tax.

I declare under penalty of perjury under the laws of California that the foregoing is true and correct.

_____

Grantor

Date: _____ _____, California

_____

Grantor

Date: _____ _____, California

If there is only one unmarried owner, it's good to add "an unmarried person" after his name to show that a spouse wasn't mistakenly left out of the document. When there is more than one owner, you should designate how they hold title now, like this: "Corrine W. Albertson and Ian R. Mayer, joint tenants." As discussed in Chapter 2, if any of the current owners are married or have entered into a registered domestic partnership, their spouses should sign the deed with them.

If there is a possibility of confusion about someone's name—for example, if the grantor took possession of the property under a different name than she is conveying it by—then all names must be included in the deed. This will make it clear that the different names refer to the same person and avoid the possibility of an apparent gap in the chain of title.

The easiest way to link the names is with "a.k.a." or "also known as." For example, if Maria Smith bought property but has since married and changed her name to Jones, the deed should identify her as "Maria Jones, a.k.a. Maria Smith."

5 Check the Words of Transfer

The words of transfer, which show the grantor's intent to convey the property to the grantee, determine what kind of deed (grant or quitclaim) you have.

The deed forms in this book already have the correct word ("grant" or "quitclaim") printed on them. Don't get creative and add your own language to the deed to make it sound like one of those impressive store-bought ones that have a whole string of terms shoehorned into them. It may not hurt in most cases, but it sure doesn't help.

6 Identify the New Owner (Grantee)

The deed must clearly identify the grantee and how he, she, they, or it (a business, for example) is taking title. The pros and cons of the various ways to take title are discussed in Chapter 3. Here are examples of the choices for the actual wording of the deed:

To an unmarried recipient: "to Henry Anderson, an unmarried man."

To co-owners in joint tenancy: "to Henry Anderson and Melanie Strauss, in joint tenancy with right of survivorship."

To co-owners as tenants in common: "to Henry Anderson and Melanie Strauss, as tenants in common."

To a married couple, as community property with right of survivorship: "to Henry Anderson and Melanie Anderson, as community property with right of survivorship."

To a married couple as regular community property: "to Henry Anderson and Melanie Anderson, husband and wife, as community property."

To registered domestic partners as regular community property: "to Henry Anderson and Robert Ishikawa, registered domestic partners, as community property."

To a living trust: "to Joan Goodman, trustee of the Joan Goodman Revocable Living Trust dated May 28, 1992."

To a minor under the Uniform Transfers to Minors Act: "to Joan Goodman, as custodian for Henry Anderson until age 22, under the California Uniform Transfers to Minors Act."

To a partnership: "to Elm Street Books, a partnership."

To a corporation: "to Anderson Enterprises, Inc., a California corporation."

To a limited liability company: "to Blocks and Blocks, a California limited liability company."

Here are some special considerations:

- **Multiple grantees.** If you name more than one grantee, each is presumed to get an equal interest in the property unless the deed specifies different shares.

  EXAMPLE 1: A deed "to Reuben Gerber and Elizabeth Roman" gives each a half-interest in the property transferred.

  EXAMPLE 2: A deed "to Reuben Gerber, a one-third interest, and to Elizabeth Roman, a two-thirds interest, as tenants in common in the following described real property ..." gives them unequal interests. (Remember, tenancy in common is the only way to create unequal shares. Property held in joint tenancy must be shared equally by the co-owners.)

  It's allowable, but never advisable, to convey property to a class of persons— for example, "my children"—instead of naming each grantee. You're just asking for trouble, though. Even a seemingly simple term like "children" can cause confusion when stepchildren, adopted children, or out-of-wedlock children are involved. There's no reason not to name each person you want to own the property.

- **Persons who go by more than one name.** As mentioned above, if there is a chance that using only one name for a grantee will create confusion about her identity, spell out all names the grantee uses. For example, "Maria R. Smith, a.k.a. Maria Smith-Jones."

Transfer to One Owner

Recording requested by

David North
46 Casey Way
San Francisco, CA 94122

and when recorded mail
this deed and tax statements to

same as above

| | For recorder's use |

Grant Deed

☐ This transfer is exempt from the documentary transfer tax.

☑ The documentary transfer tax is $ ___200.00___ and is computed on:

☐ the full value of the interest or property conveyed.

☑ the full value less the value of liens or encumbrances remaining thereon at the time of sale.

The property is located in ☐ an unincorporated area. ☑ the city of ___San Francisco___

For a valuable consideration, receipt of which is hereby acknowledged, ___Marta A. Richardson and David___ ___North, tenants in common,___ hereby grant(s) to ___David North, an___ ___unmarried man,___

the following real property in the City of ___San Francisco___, County of ___San Francisco___ California:

Beginning at a point on the easterly line of Casey Way, distant thereon 200 feet south from the south line of 4th Avenue; thence south and along said line of Casey Way 25 feet; thence at a right angle east 130 feet; thence at a right angle north 25 feet; thence at a right angle west 130 feet to the point of beginning.

Being a part of Outside Land Block No. 440.

Date: ___June 14, 20xx___   *David North*

Date: ___June 14, 20xx___   *Marta A. Richardson*

Date: _____

Date: _____

State of California

County of ___San Francisco___   }

On ___June 14, 20xx___, before me, ___Kimberly Johnson___,

a notary public in and for said state, personally appeared ___David North and Marta A. Richardson___,

personally known to me (or proved to me on the basis of satisfactory evidence) to be the person(s) whose name(s) is/are subscribed to the within instrument, and acknowledged to me that he/she/they executed the same in his/her/their authorized capacity(ies) and that by his/her/their signature(s) on the instrument the person(s), or entity upon behalf of which the person(s) acted, executed the instrument.

Kimberly Johnson   [SEAL]
Signature of Notary

Transfer to Living Trust

Recording requested by

Walter Sinclair and Eve Sinclair
8714 Hayes Street
Pasadena, California 92408

and when recorded mail
this deed and tax statements to

same as above

For recorder's use

Grant Deed

☑ This transfer is exempt from the documentary transfer tax.

☐ The documentary transfer tax is $_____ and is computed on:

    ☐ the full value of the interest or property conveyed.

    ☑ the full value less the value of liens or encumbrances remaining thereon at the time of sale.

The property is located in ☐ an unincorporated area. ☑ the city of ___Pasadena___

For a valuable consideration, receipt of which is hereby acknowledged, ___Alexander Sinclair and Emma Sinclair,___ ___husband and wife___ hereby grant(s) to ___Alexander Sinclair and___ ___Eve Sinclair, trustees of the Walter Sinclair and Eve Sinclair Revocable Living Trust dated July 2, 2002,___

the following real property in the City of ___Pasadena___, County of ___Los Angeles___ California:

    Portion of Lots 14 and 15, Block 3, of the Del Mar Tract, filed March 21, 1934, Map Book B, page 187, Los Angeles County records, described as follows:

    Beginning on the east line of Powell Street, distant thereon from the point of beginning north 0°45' east along Powell Street 60 feet; thence southeast along the south line of Clay Street 113 feet to the point of beginning.

Date: _July 19, 20xx_   _Emma Sinclair_

Date: _July 19, 20xx_   _Alexander Sinclair_

Date: _____   _____

Date: _____   _____

State of California

County of ___Los Angeles___ }

On ___July 19, 20xx___, before me, ___Kimberly Johnson___,

a notary public in and for said state, personally appeared ___Emma Sinclair and Alexander Sinclair___,

personally known to me (or proved to me on the basis of satisfactory evidence) to be the person(s) whose name(s) is/are subscribed to the within instrument, and acknowledged to me that he/she/they executed the same in his/her/their authorized capacity(ies) and that by his/her/their signature(s) on the instrument the person(s), or entity upon behalf of which the person(s) acted, executed the instrument.

Kimberly Johnson
Signature of Notary   [SEAL]

7 Enter a Physical Description of the Property

Obviously, a deed must identify the property being transferred. Your description should start with the city (if the property isn't inside a city's limits, cross out "City of") and the county in which the property is located.

Next, on to the specific description. In almost every case you can simply copy the legal description from the old deed. If there isn't enough room on the deed to get the whole thing, type "See description on Attachment 1" in the space. Then either photocopy the old legal description or type it on a separate plain piece of paper, and label it, for example, "Attachment 1 to grant deed from Sonia O'Toole to Kyle Garrett, April 2, 20xx," and staple it to the deed. To be extra careful, the grantor can sign the attachment page as well as the deed.

If you retype the legal description (which may contain lots of strange-looking numbers and symbols), be very careful not to make a transcription error. Check it by having someone read out loud from the old deed while you follow along on the new one.

If the current owner can't find his deed, you should be able to get a copy of it from the county recorder's office (if, of course, it was recorded). If the recorder can't come up with a deed, this is a red flag—a possible break in the chain of title discussed in Chapter 1—warning you that something is very wrong. You should talk to someone at a title company or a lawyer.

You will need a new legal description if:

- you have reason to think that the old deed's description is erroneous, or
- you are transferring only part of the property described in the old deed.

In almost all cases, you will want to hire a surveyor or real estate professional to help you with this. If you don't need to get a new description for your property, you can skip the rest of this section.

There are four main ways property can be described, although no particular kind of description is required by statute. The general rule is that the description must be adequate to allow a surveyor to identify the land. It must, however, specify the county as well as the city; California statute (Civ. Code § 1092) requires it.

(1) Metes and bounds. The first method is called "metes and bounds," an old term meaning measures and directions. A metes and bounds description describes the perimeter of the property. The description must thus start at an identifiable point and end there as well. Below is an example that refers to a map recorded in San Francisco.

Sample Metes and Bounds Description

ORDER NO. 220-596-2

City & SAN FRANCISCO,

The land referred to in this Report is situated in the State of California, County of and is described as follows:

BEGINNING at a point on the northerly line of Geary Boulevard, formerly Geary Street, distant thereon 75 feet easterly from the easterly line of 44th Avenue; running thence northerly at right angles to said line of Geary Boulevard 90 feet, 1-1/4 inches to the southerly line of Point Lobos Avenue; thence easterly along said line of Point Lobos Avenue 31 feet, 10 inches; thence southerly 86 feet, 3/4 of an inch to a point on said northerly line of Geary Boulevard, distant thereon 92 feet, 4-3/8 inches easterly from the said easterly line of 44th Avenue; thence westerly along said line of Geary Boulevard 17 feet, 4-3/8 inches to the point of beginning.

BEING a portion of OUTSIDE LAND BLOCK NO. 224.

Order No. 49333 PC

EXHIBIT "A" AS REFERRED TO IN THE DEED FROM DAVID MACLEAN TO
REAL PROPERTIES, INC., a California corporation dated 9/17/84

The land referred to in this Report is situated in the State of California, County of Contra Costa
                                                  and is described as follows:
City of Richmond

Portion of Lots 11 and 13, Block 19, map of the San Pablo Villa Tract, filed September
21, 1905, Map Book C, page 65, Contra Costa County Records, described as follows:

Beginning on the east line of Hayes Street, formerly Powell Street, distant thereon
north 0 degrees 45' west 59 feet from the southwest corner of said Block 19; thence
from said point of beginning north 0 degrees 45' east along the east line of Hayes
Street 41.5 feet; thence southeasterly parallel with the south line of Emeric Avenue,
formerly Clay Street 112.5 feet to the west line of Lot 12; thence southerly along
said line 41.5 feet; thence northwesterly parallel with the south line of Emeric
Avenue 112.5 feet to the point of beginning.

BOOK 11983 PAGE 203

84 137602

END OF DOCUMENT

(2) Township/Range. The second way of describing property is based on a survey system that divides the state into a grid. The north-south lines are called ranges, and the east-west lines are called townships. The starting place for a description of this kind is always one of the three north-south lines in California that are designated as "principal meridians." The space on the grid where the property is located is identified by counting from a principal meridian. Each space on the grid east or west of a principal meridian counts as one range. Confused? It gets worse. Each space on the grid created by township and range lines is divided into 36 one-square mile sections. It's easier to understand by looking at the diagram below:

Township/Range System

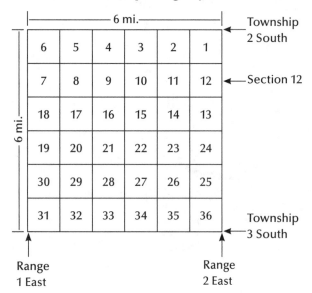

(3) Reference to a recorded map. The third way to describe property is much simpler and, of course, less common. It is simply a reference to an approved subdivision map or official city or county map that has been recorded with the county. The recorded map (also called a plat) will have the township and range coordinates on it.

> **EXAMPLE:** "Parcel 35 of Country View Estates, a duly recorded subdivision, a map of which was recorded in the Contra Costa County plat books at book 498, page 1213, on January 14, 1986."

(4) Name of the property. It is also permissible to refer to a piece of property by name, if it's generally known that way. (Civ. Code § 1092.) If, for example, you are transferring the "Cartwright Ranch," and everyone will know what property that means, you're all right. Generally, though, you are better off to refer to a surveyor's description, either by including a metes and bounds or township/range description or by referring to a recorded map. It's just more concrete and less likely to cause problems later on.

You may have noticed that none of these ways of describing land pays much attention to the number of square feet or acres in the property. If the number of acres is specified and doesn't agree with a more certain (for example, metes and bounds) description, the more definite description prevails.

8 List Encumbrances

As discussed above, unless a grant deed says otherwise, the law presumes that the interest transferred by these deeds is not encumbered (for example, by taxes, assessments, liens, or mortgages) except to the extent that the grantor has disclosed. Quitclaim deeds, on the other hand, only transfer whatever interest the grantor owns and are free of presumptions.

Accordingly, a grant deed should clearly identify all encumbrances. If it doesn't, the grantee can sue either for rescission (cancellation) of the sale or for the difference between what he paid for the property and its actual value taking into account the encumbrances.

9 Add Covenants, If Necessary

When real property is transferred, restrictions on its use sometimes go with it. These restrictions, called "covenants running with the land," may be spelled out in the deed, but more commonly are recorded separately. Only covenants that relate to use of the property may run with the land. Examples are covenants to pay rent, to pay taxes, or to ensure "quiet enjoyment" of the property. (Civ. Code §§ 1460 and following.) A covenant not related to the land—

say, to belong to a certain church or give money to someone—will not be enforced.

Most people have no need to include covenants in a deed that simply transfers ownership within a family or changes the way title is held. These days covenants are most commonly used by homeowners' associations in subdivisions or condominium complexes. The grantee takes the property subject to a set of "conditions, covenants and restrictions," which is recorded in the county recorder's office. You can't eliminate these.

The restrictions can be quite detailed, covering everything from what color you can paint your house to what kind of fences, outbuildings, or pets you are allowed to have. Obviously, they can be quite important to anyone thinking of living there. Any prospective owner should get a complete copy of the restrictions, which the homeowners' association must provide upon request, before the transfer.

Racial covenants, which prohibited use of land by minorities, were shockingly common until the Supreme Court ruled them unenforceable in 1948. (*Shelley v. Kraemer,* 334 U.S. 1 (1948).) State law now voids covenants that directly or indirectly restrict the use or acquisition of property based on a person's sex, race, color, religion, ancestry, ethnic group, or national origin. (Civ. Code §§ 53, 782.) Nonetheless, they persist in the records, impotent but ugly reminders of bigotry. Some deeds signed today still refer to covenants like the one shown below, which is recorded in the Contra Costa County Recorder's office.

If a legally enforceable covenant is violated, the injured party can sue the owner and collect money damages. The transfer of the property isn't affected; the grantor can't take the property back.

10 Sign and Date the Deed

This usually is straightforward enough. The important thing to remember is that all owners of the property being transferred, and their spouses, must sign the deed. The deed isn't binding on any who don't sign. See Chapter 2 for the rules that govern who must

sign the deed when a business transfers property or if you're signing under a power of attorney.

Grantors should sign their names exactly as they are typed or printed on the deed.

11 Get the Signatures Notarized

The acknowledgment of the grantor's signature on a deed is formal proof that the signature is genuine. The grantor states, before a notary public, that he is the person whose signature appears on the deed, and the notary signs a statement to that effect. Notarization has nothing to do with the substance of the deed or the grantor's title to the property being transferred.

Notarization of the signature on a deed is not required for the deed's validity. As long as you sign a deed that contains all the elements set out above, the deed is legal and binding on the parties. Acknowledgment, however, is required if you want to record your deed with the county recorder—which you do (Chapter 6 discusses the recording system). We include the mechanics of completing the notarization here for convenience, because you will want to fill out the acknowledgment part of the deed when you sign it. After the deed is signed and notarized, go to Chapter 6.

If the Grantor Is in California

A notary public can acknowledge a signature anywhere in the state. You can usually find a notary in a bank, real estate agency, or lawyer's office. Other public officials can acknowledge a signature in the county or city in which they are elected or appointed: a municipal or justice court judge or clerk, county or city clerk, court commissioner, district or city attorney, county counsel, or clerk of a board of supervisors. (Civ. Code § 1181.)

California notaries public must keep a journal of all their official notarial acts, and you must sign it when your signature is notarized. If you're signing a deed (except a deed of reconveyance), you must also put your thumbprint in the journal; this requirement is to combat forgery. (Gov't. Code § 8206.)

An Illegal Racial Covenant

...delivery of these presents, the receipt whereof is hereby acknowledged, has granted, bargained, sold and conveyed, and by these presents do grant, bargain, sell and convey unto said parties of the second part, and to their heirs and assigns forever,

ALL that certain real property, situated in the County of Contra Costa, State of California, and bounded and particularly described as follows, to-wit:

Lot Numbered Forty-three (43) as said lot is shown upon that certain map entitled, "Kensington Terrace, Contra Costa County, California, July 1926" - filed in the office of the County Recorder of the said County of Contra Costa, September 10, 1926 in Book 20 of Maps, at pages 519 and 520.

The property hereinabove described is conveyed and this deed is accepted pursuant to the following convenants, conditions and restrictions, which shall, as to each and every part thereof, apply to and be binding upon the said parties of the second part, their heirs and assigns, viz:

1. That no building other than a dwelling house shall be constructed upon the property herein described, and that no building used for dwelling purposes shall be constructed of a less value than $3500.00, provided, however, that the usual garage and outbuildings may be constructed as appurtenant to said residence.

2. That neither said real property nor any interest therein nor any improvements thereon shall ever be used or occupied by any person of African, Mongolian, Chinese or Japanese descent, except as a servant of the then owner or occupant thereof.

If the Grantor Is Outside California

A grantor who is outside the state can have his or her signature verified by a notary public for that state, or by anyone else authorized by that state to take acknowledgments. If the grantor is outside the country, certain diplomatic personnel and foreign judges and notaries may take the acknowledgment:

- a minister, commissioner, or chargé d'affaires of the United States, resident and accredited in the country where the proof or acknowledgment is made
- a consul, vice consul, or consular agent of the United States, resident in the country where the proof or acknowledgment is made
- a judge of a court of record of the country where the proof or acknowledgment is made
- commissioners appointed by the governor or secretary of state for that purpose, or

- a notary public. (But the notary's signature must itself be acknowledged before a judge or American diplomatic or consular officer. Civ. Code § 1183.)

No matter where the deed is signed, the grantor should use the acknowledgment form approved by California (the one on the form deeds in this book). Otherwise a California county recorder may not want to accept the deed for recording.

If the Grantor Is in the Armed Services

There are also special rules for members of the armed services. Officers who have the powers of a notary public can notarize documents for any service members, in the United States or out; outside the country, they can also notarize documents for spouses of persons serving in the armed forces or employees of the services. A sample declaration is shown below; a tear-out copy is in the appendix.

Form for Acknowledgment: Military Personnel

On this the _____ day of _____, _____, before me, _____, the undersigned officer, personally appeared _____, known to me (or satisfactorily proven) to be (a) serving in the armed forces of the United States, (b) a spouse of a person serving in the armed forces of the United States, or (c) a person serving with, employed by, or accompanying the armed forces of the United States outside the United States and outside the Canal Zone, Puerto Rico, Guam, and the Virgin Islands, and to be the person whose name is subscribed to the within instrument and acknowledged that he executed the same. And the undersigned does further certify that he is at the date of this certificate a commissioned officer in the active service of the armed forces of the United States having the general powers of a notary public under the provisions of Section 936 of Title 10 of the United States Code (Public Law 90-632).

_____
Signature of officer

_____
Rank

_____
Capacity in which signed

Serial number

Branch of service

If Acknowledgment Is Impossible

If for some reason you have a deed that cannot be acknowledged by the grantor himself—if, for example, the grantor signed the deed years ago but never acknowledged it and is now unavailable—you may still be able to record the deed by following one of the procedures below. (If the grantor can acknowledge the deed, you can skip this section.)

Witnesses

In rare instances, the signing of the deed may have been witnessed. A witness who signed a trustee's deed or a deed of reconveyance—but not a grant deed, quitclaim deed, or deed of trust—may execute a document proving that the person whose name is signed to the deed as grantor actually signed the deed and that the witness also signed the deed. (Civ. Code § 1195.)

Handwriting verification

If no witnesses are available, proof of the execution of the deed may be made by verification of the handwriting of the grantor. Witnesses and parties are considered unavailable if they are nonresidents of California, if they cannot be found, or if they refuse to testify. (Civ. Code § 1198.)

To prove the grantor's handwriting, someone must sign a statement to the effect that he knew the grantor and his handwriting (and the witnesses who signed the deed, if any, and their handwriting) and that the signature is genuine. (Civ. Code § 1199.) Like an acknowledgment, this statement must be made before a notary public or one of the other persons authorized by statute.

Deliver the Deed

A deed doesn't take effect unless it is delivered to and accepted by the grantee. Basically, the law considers a deed delivered if the parties agree when the deed is signed that it is delivered, even if it is not actually in the grantee's possession.

Recording the deed or physically delivering it to the grantee also satisfies the delivery requirement.

Delivery to an agent of the grantee, or to someone acting with the grantee's permission, is also sufficient. (Civ. Code § 1059.) Delivery to one joint owner is sufficient.

A deed is presumed to have been delivered on the date it is properly executed (Civ. Code §§ 1054, 1055). This presumption applies only to the date, not the fact, of delivery—that is, if the deed was in fact delivered, the statute presumes that the date of delivery is the date the deed was signed.

Normally, the delivery requirement is no problem. Sometimes, however, people get into trouble because they try to use a deed as a substitute for a will. For example, someone wanting to leave real estate at his death may sign a deed but not record it, and lock it away in a drawer, expecting that it will be found and take effect at his death. After the person dies, the deed is discovered—but it isn't valid. In California, only a valid will, trust, or pay-on-death designation can transfer property at death, and a deed doesn't qualify as any of these.

Checklist for Preparing a Grant or Quitclaim Deed

Does the deed:

☐ contain required tax and recording information

☐ identify the grantor(s) (and their spouses)

☐ identify the grantee(s)

☐ have the right words of transfer ("grant" or "quitclaim"), and

☐ describe the property accurately and completely?

Was the deed:

☐ signed by the grantor(s) and their spouses

☐ dated

☐ notarized, and

☐ delivered" to the grantee?

Revoking a Deed

A deed is irrevocable. If you change your mind after you sign and deliver a deed, you're out of luck. On the bright side, this means that if you lose a recorded deed, there's no problem except inconvenience. You can get a certified copy from the county recorder.

If the person you transferred the property to agrees to transfer it back to you or to someone else, she must execute a new deed complying with the same formalities as the first one. Making an oral agreement, or just tearing up a deed that has been recorded, has no legal effect.

If you transferred the property to a revocable living trust, you can revoke the trust and have the trustee (who may be yourself) transfer the property back to you.

■

Chapter 6

Recording Your Deed

Once you've completed the right deed for your transfer, you should be able to relax, right? Absolutely not. You still should record the deed with the county recorder. But take heart—recording is the last hoop you have to jump through when you're dealing with a real estate transaction, and it's not at all difficult.

Recording Other Documents

Any document (not just deeds) that may affect the title to real property should be recorded. For example, an agreement between a married couple as to the community property status of real estate owned by one or both of them, an affidavit of death of a joint tenant, or a power of attorney that gives the attorney-in-fact authority to sign deeds, should be recorded.

Recording a deed really is a simple process, but you need to do more than just take your deed to the county recorder's office. Before the recorder will accept your deed for recording, you must pay the documentary transfer tax, if applicable (see Chapter 5) and file a change of ownership report. These steps are discussed next.

Step 1: Prepare Change of Ownership Forms

Two distinct forms, confusingly titled "Preliminary Change of Ownership Report" and "Change of Ownership Statement," exist to notify local property tax assessors of real estate transfers that may require a reassessment for tax purposes. All information you supply on the forms is confidential; the county will not disclose it or make it a public record. (Rev. & Tax. Code § 481.)

All transfers require the "preliminary" form, which must be filed when the deed is recorded. If you don't file it, the county assessor will send you the Change of Ownership Statement.

Preliminary Change of Ownership Report

All documents that reflect a transfer of real property must be accompanied by a "Preliminary Change of Ownership Report" when they are recorded. (Rev. & Tax. Code § 480.3.) The recorder takes the form and sends it on to the assessor. If you don't turn it in with the deed, you are liable for an extra $20 fee (unless the new owner is not a California resident) and will have to fill out and file a "Change of Ownership Statement."

Each county has its own form, although the information requested is exactly the same. You can get copies from the recorder's office or the county assessor's office. Many counties now make the form available online.

The form asks for basic information about the property and the transfer. Item 1 asks a series of questions to determine if the transfer is a "change of ownership," as defined by statute, making it subject to reappraisal by the county assessor for property tax purposes. (Property tax reassessment is discussed in Chapter 1.)

If the transfer falls into any of the categories listed in Item 1, it is exempt and you need not fill in any of the detailed transfer information (sales price, loan information, etc.) that is asked for on the rest of the form. If it is not exempt, you will have to fill out the rest of the preliminary form.

This form should be easy to fill out after reading this book. If you have questions, check the earlier discussions of ways of holding title (Chapter 3) and tax reassessment (Chapter 1), or ask the clerk at the county recorder's office.

Change of Ownership Statement

A Change of Ownership Statement, which is handled by the county assessor's office (not the county recorder), is required only when the property must be reassessed for property tax purposes or if you don't turn in a Preliminary Change of Ownership Report. (Rev. & Tax. Code § 480.) The assessor decides, based on the information in the Preliminary Report, whether or not you need to file one. If you

How the Recording System Works

The recording system is designed to keep track, in public records, of who owns every square inch of land in California. Each county has a county recorder's office, where copies of all deeds (and other documents affecting title) to property in the county are collected and indexed. Usually, deeds are indexed by name of the owners (all parties to a deed—grantors and grantees—are indexed). This means you have to look up a specific person instead of the property.

Keeping these records of all property transfers in one place allows a prospective buyer to find out just who owns property, how much it is mortgaged for, and if it is subject to any other encumbrances or restrictions (a trust deed or lien, for example). The whole idea is to have one place, the county recorder's office, where buyers can look up their property and be sure they have found all documents that affect title to it. (Usually, professional title searchers do the looking. Title searches and title insurance are discussed in Chapter 1.)

Here are the basic rules:

- If a deed is recorded, the law presumes that everyone knows about (or should know about) it.

EXAMPLE: Helga buys a piece of property that is subject to a recorded easement. She is deemed to know about the easement— even though she doesn't. (She should have looked it up.)

- If a deed is not recorded, the transfer is still valid and binding on the people directly involved and on anyone who actually knows about it.

EXAMPLE: Kim sells a piece of property to Mark. Robin knows about the sale but also knows that Mark hasn't recorded the deed. She buys the same property from Kim and runs down to record her deed first. She gets to the county recorder before Mark does. Mark's deed still stands. The recording statute does not protect Robin, who bought the property knowing that it had already been sold to someone else. (Kim may also be in trouble. It's a criminal offense to sell, with the intent to defraud, the same piece of land twice. See Penal Code § 533.)

- If a deed is not recorded, it is not binding on someone who buys the property later with no knowledge of the earlier deed.

EXAMPLE: Ruth gives her house to her daughter Vera, but Vera doesn't record the deed. After Ruth dies, her husband inherits the property and sells it to Ray. Neither the husband nor Ray knows about the previous deed to Vera (it wasn't recorded, and they didn't find out any other way). When Ray records the deed, he is the legal owner of the property; his deed takes precedence over Vera's.

GREGORY J. SMITH, SAN DIEGO COUNTY ASSESSOR / RECORDER / CLERK
1600 PACIFIC HIGHWAY, ROOM 103 · SAN DIEGO, CALIFORNIA 92101-2480
TELEPHONE (619) 531-5848

PRELIMINARY CHANGE OF OWNERSHIP REPORT

[To be completed by transferee (buyer) prior to transfer of subject property in accordance with section 480.3 of the Revenue and Taxation Code.] A Preliminary Change in Ownership Report must be filed with each conveyance in the County Recorder's office for the county where the property is located; this particular form may be used in all 58 counties.

THIS REPORT IS NOT A PUBLIC DOCUMENT

SELLER/TRANSFEROR: _____

BUYER/TRANSFEREE: _____

ASSESSOR'S PARCEL NUMBER(S): _____

PROPERTY ADDRESS OR LOCATION: _____

MAIL TAX INFORMATION TO: Name_____

              Address _____

            Phone Number (8 a.m. to 5 p.m.) (_____)_____

FOR RECORDER'S USE ONLY	
NV-O	NV-T
CSH	PP
AREA	

NOTICE: A lien for property taxes applies to your property on January 1 of each year for the taxes owing in the following fiscal year, July 1 through June 30. One-half of these taxes is due November 1, and one-half is due February 1. The first installment becomes delinquent on December 10, and the second installment becomes delinquent on April 10. One tax bill is mailed before November 1 to the owner of record. **You may be responsible for the current or upcoming property taxes even if you do not receive the tax bill.**

The property which you acquired may be subject to a supplemental assessment in an amount to be determined by the San Diego County Assessor. For further information on your supplemental roll obligation, please call the Assessor Realty Division at (858) 505-6262. For information about this form, please call the Change in Ownership Section at (619) 531-5848.

PART I: TRANSFER INFORMATION *(please answer all questions)*

Yes No

☐ ☐ A. Is this transfer solely between husband and wife (addition of a spouse, death of a spouse, divorce settlement, etc.)?

☐ ☐ B. Is this transaction only a correction of the name(s) of the person(s) holding title to the property (for example, a name change upon marriage)?
Please explain _____

☐ ☐ C. Is this document recorded to create, terminate or reconvey a lender's interest in the property?

☐ ☐ D. Is this transaction recorded only as a requirement for financing purposes or to create, terminate or reconvey a security interest (e.g., cosigner)? Please explain _____

☐ ☐ E. Is this document recorded to substitute a trustee of a trust, mortgage or other similar document?

☐ ☐ F. Did this transfer result in the creation of a joint tenancy in which the seller (transferor) remains as one of the joint tenants?

☐ ☐ G. Does this transfer return property to the person who created the joint tenancy (original transferor)?

      H. Is this transfer of property:

☐ ☐   1. to a revocable trust that may be revoked by the transferor and is for the benefit of the ☐ transferor ☐ transferor's spouse?

☐ ☐   2. to a trust that may be revoked by the Creator/Grantor who is also a joint tenant, and which names the other joint tenant(s) as beneficiaries when the Creator/Grantor dies?

☐ ☐   3. to an irrevocable trust for the benefit of the ☐ Creator/Grantor and/or ☐ Grantor's spouse?

☐ ☐   4. to an irrevocable trust from which the property reverts to the Creator/Grantor within 12 years?

☐ ☐ I. If this property is subject to a lease, is the remaining lease term 35 years or more including written options?

☐ ☐*J. Is this a transfer between ☐ parent(s) and child(ren)? ☐ or from grandparent(s) to grandchild(ren)?

☐ ☐*K. Is this transaction to replace a principal residence by a person 55 years of age or older? Within the same county? ☐ Yes ☐ No

☐ ☐*L. Is this transaction to replace a principal residence by a person who is severely disabled as defined by Revenue and Taxation Code Section 69.5? Within the same county? ☐ Yes ☐ No

☐ ☐ M. Is this transfer solely between domestic partners currently registered with the California Secretary of State?

*If you checked yes to J, K or L, you may qualify for a property tax reassessment exclusion, which may result in lower taxes on your property. **If you do not file a claim, your property will be reassessed.**

Please provide any other information that will help the Assessor to understand the nature of the transfer.

If the conveying document constitutes an exclusion from a change in ownership as defined in section 62 of the Revenue and Taxation Code for any reason other than those listed above, set forth this specific exclusions claimed: _____

Please answer all questions in each section. If a question does not apply, indicate with "N/A". Sign and date at bottom of second page.

PART II: OTHER TRANSFER INFORMATION

A. Date of transfer if other than recording date _____.

B. Type of transfer. *(Please check appropriate box.)*

☐ Purchase ☐ Foreclosure   ☐ Gift ☐ Trade or Exchange   ☐ Merger, Stock or Partnership Acquisition

☐ Contract of Sale – Date of Contract _____

☐ Inheritance – Date of Death _____ ☐ Other *(Please explain):* _____

☐ Creation of a Lease   ☐ Assignment of a Lease   ☐ Termination of a Lease   ☐ Sale/Leaseback

☐ Date Lease began _____

☐ Original term in years (including written options) _____

☐ Remaining term in years (including written options) _____

    Monthly Payment _____ Remaining Term _____

C. Was only a partial interest in the property transferred? ☐ Yes ☐ No

    If **yes**, indicate the percentage transferred _____%.

BOE-502-A (FRONT) REV. 8 (10-05)

Please answer, to the best of your knowledge, all applicable questions, then sign and date. If a question does not apply, indicate with "N/A".

PART III: PURCHASE PRICE AND TERMS OF SALE

A.   CASH DOWN PAYMENT OR value of trade or exchange *(excluding closing costs)*   Amount $ _____

B.   FIRST DEED OF TRUST @ _____ % interest for _____ years. Pymts./Mo. = $ _____ (Prin. & Int. Only) Amount $ _____
☐ FHA (_____ Discount Points)   ☐ Fixed Rate   ☐ New Loan
☐ Conventional   ☐ Variable Rate   ☐ Assumed Existing Loan Balance
☐ VA (_____ Discount Points)   ☐ All inclusive D. T. ($_____ Wrapped)   ☐ Bank or Savings & Loan
☐ Cal-Vet   ☐ Loan Carried by Seller   ☐ Finance Company
Balloon Payment   ☐ Yes ☐ No   Due Date _____   Amount $ _____

C.   SECOND DEED OF TRUST @ _____ % interest for _____ years. Pymts./Mo. = $ _____ (Prin. & Int. Only) Amount $ _____
☐ Bank or Savings & Loan   ☐ Fixed Rate   ☐ New Loan
☐ Loan Carried by Seller   ☐ Variable Rate   ☐ Assumed Existing Loan Balance
Balloon Payment   ☐ Yes ☐ No   Due Date _____   Amount $ _____

D.   OTHER FINANCING: Is other financing involved not covered in (b) or (c) above?   ☐ Yes ☐ No   Amount $ _____
Type _____ @ _____ % interest for _____ years. Pymts./Mo. = $ _____ (Prin. & Int.Only)
☐ Bank or Savings & Loan   ☐ Fixed Rate   ☐ New Loan
☐ Loan Carried by Seller   ☐ Variable Rate   ☐ Assumed Existing Loan Balance
Balloon Payment   ☐ Yes ☐ No   Due Date _____   Amount $ _____

E.   WAS AN IMPROVEMENT BOND ASSUMED BY THE BUYER?   ☐ Yes ☐ No   Outstanding Balance: Amount $ _____

F.   TOTAL PURCHASE PRICE *(or acquisition price, if traded or exchanged, include real estate commission if paid.)*
                                        TOTAL ITEMS A THROUGH E $ _____

G.   PROPERTY PURCHASED ☐ Through a broker ☐ Direct from Seller ☐ From a family member ☐ Other *(please explain)*:_____
If purchased through a broker, provide broker's name and phone number: _____
Please explain any special terms, seller concessions, or financing and any other information that would help the Assessor understand the purchase
price and terms of sale. _____

PART IV: PROPERTY INFORMATION

A.   TYPE OF PROPERTY TRANSFERRED:
☐ Single – family residence   ☐ Agricultural   ☐ Timeshare
☐ Multiple – family residence (no. of units: _____)   ☐ Co-op/Own-your-own   ☐ Manufactured Home
☐ Commercial/Industrial   ☐ Condominium   ☐ Unimproved Lot
☐ Other (Description: i.e., timber, mineral, water rights, etc.) _____

B.   IS THIS PROPERTY INTENDED AS YOUR PRINCIPAL RESIDENCE?   ☐ Yes ☐ No
If **yes**, enter date of occupancy _____ / _____, 20_____ or intended occupancy _____ / _____, 20_____.
                                    (month)   (day)   (year)   (month)   (day)   (year)

C.   IS PERSONAL PROPERTY INCLUDED IN THE PURCHASE PRICE (i.e., furniture, farm equipment, machinery, etc.)?
(other than a manufactured home subject to local property tax?)   ☐ Yes ☐ No
If **yes**, enter the value of the personal property included in the purchase price $ _____ *(Attach itemized list of personal property)*

D.   IS A MANUFACTURED HOME INCLUDED IN THE PURCHASE PRICE?   ☐ Yes ☐ No
If **yes**, how much of the purchase price is allocated to the manufactured home? $ _____
Is the manufactured home subject to local property tax?   ☐ Yes   ☐ No   What is the Decal Number? _____

E.   DOES THE PROPERTY PRODUCE INCOME?   ☐ Yes   ☐ No   If **yes**, is the income from:
☐ Lease/Rent   ☐ Contract   ☐ Mineral Rights   ☐ Other *(please explain)*: _____

F.   WHAT WAS THE CONDITION OF THE PROPERTY AT THE TIME OF SALE?
☐ Good   ☐ Average   ☐ Fair   ☐ Poor

Please explain the physical condition of the property and provide any other information (such as restrictions, etc.) that would assist the Assessor in
determining the value of the property: _____
_____

CERTIFICATION

OWNERSHIP TYPE (✓)
Proprietorship   ☐
Partnership   ☐   *I certify that the foregoing is true, correct and complete to the best of my knowledge and belief.*
Corporation   ☐   *This declaration is binding on each and every co-owner and/or partner.*
Other _____   ☐

NAME OF NEW OWNER/CORPORATE OFFICER	TITLE

SIGNATURE OF NEW OWNER/CORPORATE OFFICER	DATE

NAME OF ENTITY *(typed or printed)*	FEDERAL EMPLOYER ID NUMBER

ADDRESS *(typed or printed)*	E-MAIL ADDRESS *(optional)*	DATE

(NOTE: The Assessor may contact you for additional information.)
If a document evidencing a change of ownership is presented to the recorder for recordation without the concurrent filing of a preliminary
change of ownership report, the recorder may charge an additional recording fee of twenty dollars ($20).

BOE-502-A (BACK) REV. 8 (10-05)

BOE-502-AH (FRONT) REV. 8 (10-05)

WEBSTER J. GUILLORY
ORANGE COUNTY ASSESSOR
CHANGE OF OWNERSHIP STATEMENT
REAL PROPERTY OR MANUFACTURED HOMES
SUBJECT TO LOCAL PROPERTY TAXES

RECORDING DATA
Date _____
Document Number _____
Book _____ Page_____

County of ORANGE, Office of Assessor
Address: P.O. BOX 1948   SANTA ANA, CA 92702-1948
Telephone: (714) 834-5031
Correct mailing address if necessary.
Name and Address of Buyer/Transferee *[last name, first name(s), initial]*

File This Statement By _____

Assessor's Parcel Number _____

Property Address _____

_____

_____

Legal Description _____

_____

_____

Seller/Transferor _____
(Last name, first name(s), initial)

Phone No. (8 a.m.–5 p.m.) (____)

IMPORTANT NOTICE

The law requires any transferee acquiring an interest in real property or manufactured home subject to local property taxation, and that is assessed by the Assessor, to file a Change of Ownership Statement with the County Recorder or Assessor. The Change of Ownership Statement must be filed at the time of recording or, if the transfer is not recorded, within 45 days of the date of the change in ownership, except that where the change in ownership has occurred by reason of death the statement shall be filed within 150 days after the date of death or, if the estate is probated, shall be filed at the time the inventory and appraisal is filed. The failure to file a change in ownership statement within 45 days from the date of a written request by the Assessor results in a penalty of either: (1) One hundred dollars ($100), or (2) 10 percent of the taxes applicable to the new base year value reflecting the change in ownership of the real property or manufactured home, whichever is greater, but not to exceed two thousand five hundred dollars ($2,500) if that failure to file was not willful. This penalty will be added to the assessment roll and shall be collected like any other delinquent property taxes, and be subject to the same penalties for nonpayment.

This notice is a written request from the Office of the Assessor for a Change of Ownership Statement. If you do not file this statement, it will result in the assessment of a penalty. This statement will be held secret as required by section 481 of the Revenue and Taxation Code.

The property which you acquired may be subject to a supplemental assessment in an amount to be determined by the ORANGE COUNTY Assessor. For further information on your supplemental roll obligation, please call the ORANGE COUNTY ASSESSOR at (714) 834-2941

PART I: TRANSFER INFORMATION *(Please answer all questions.)*

YES   NO

☐   ☐   A. Is this transfer solely between husband and wife (addition of a spouse, death of a spouse, divorce settlement, etc.)?

☐   ☐   B. Is this transaction only a correction of the name(s) of the person(s) holding title to the property (e.g., a name change upon marriage)?
Please explain: _____

☐   ☐   C. Is this document recorded to create, terminate, or reconvey a lender's interest in the property?

☐   ☐   D. Is this transaction recorded only as a requirement for financing purposes or to create, terminate, or reconvey a security interest (e.g., cosigner)? Please explain: _____

☐   ☐   E. Is this document recorded to substitute a trustee of a trust, mortgage, or other similar document?

☐   ☐   F. Did this transfer result in the creation of a joint tenancy in which the seller (transferor) remains as one of the joint tenants?

☐   ☐   G. Does this transfer return property to the person who created the joint tenancy (original transferor)?

☐   ☐   H. Is this transfer of property:

☐   ☐   1. to a revocable trust that may be revoked by the transferor and is for the benefit of the ☐ transferor ☐ transferor's spouse?

☐   ☐   2. to a trust that may be revoked by the Creator/Grantor who is also a joint tenant, and which names the other joint tenant(s) as beneficiaries when the Creator/Grantor dies?

☐   ☐   3. to an irrevocable trust for the benefit of the ☐ Creator/Grantor and/or ☐ Grantor's spouse?

☐   ☐   4. to an irrevocable trust from which the property reverts to the Creator/Grantor within 12 years?

☐   ☐   I. If this property is subject to a lease, is the remaining lease term 35 years or more including written options?

☐   ☐   *J. Is this a transfer between parent(s) and child(ren)? ☐Yes ☐No or from grandparent(s) to grandchild(ren)? ☐Yes ☐No

☐   ☐   *K. Is this transaction to replace a principal residence by a person 55 years of age or older?   Within the same county?   ☐Yes ☐No

☐   ☐   *L. Is this transaction to replace a principal residence by a person who is severely disabled as defined by Revenue and Taxation Code section 69.5? Within the same county?   ☐Yes ☐No

☐   ☐   M. Is this transfer solely between domestic partners currently registered with the California Secretary of State?

*If you answered **yes** to J, K or L, you may qualify for a property tax reassessment exclusion, which may result in lower taxes on your property. If you do not file a claim, it will result in the reassessment of the property.

Please provide any other information that will help the Assessor to understand the nature of the transfer.

IF YOU HAVE ANSWERED **YES** TO ANY OF THE ABOVE QUESTIONS **EXCEPT** J, K OR L, PLEASE SIGN AND DATE, OTHERWISE COMPLETE THE REVERSE SIDE.

➡ .A002-254 (R10/05)

BOE-502-AH (BACK) REV. 8 (10-05)

PART II: OTHER TRANSFER INFORMATION

A. Date of transfer if other than recording date _____ .

B. Type of transfer. *(Please check appropriate box.)*

☐ Purchase ☐ Foreclosure ☐ Gift ☐ Trade or exchange ☐ Merger, stock, or partnership acquisition

☐ Contract of sale — Date of contract _____ ☐ Sale/Leaseback

☐ Inheritance — Date of death _____ ☐ Other: Please explain: _____

☐ Creation of a lease ☐ Assignment of a lease ☐ Termination of a lease. Date lease began _____

☐ Original term in years (including written options) _____ Remaining term in years (including written options) _____

C. Was only a partial interest in the property transferred? ☐ Yes ☐ No If **yes**, indicate the percentage transferred _____%.

PART III: PURCHASE PRICE AND TERMS OF SALE

A. CASH DOWN PAYMENT OR VALUE OF TRADE OR EXCHANGE (excluding closing costs) — Amount $ _____

B. FIRST DEED OF TRUST @ _____% interest for _____ years. Pymts./Mo. = $ _____ *(Prin. & Int. only)* — Amount $ _____

☐ FHA (_____ Discount Points) ☐ Fixed rate ☐ New loan

☐ Conventional ☐ Variable rate ☐ Assumed existing loan balance

☐ VA (_____ Discount Points) ☐ All inclusive D.T. ($ _____ Wrapped) ☐ Bank or savings & loan

☐ Cal-Vet ☐ Loan carried by seller ☐ Finance company

Balloon payment ☐ Yes ☐ No Due Date _____ — Amount $ _____

C. SECOND DEED OF TRUST @ _____% interest for _____ years. Pymts./Mo. = $ _____ *(Prin. & Int. only)* — Amount $ _____

☐ Bank or savings & loan ☐ Fixed rate ☐ New loan

☐ Loan carried by seller ☐ Variable rate ☐ Assumed existing loan balance

Balloon payment ☐ Yes ☐ No Due Date _____ — Amount $ _____

D. OTHER FINANCING: Is other financing involved not covered in (b) or (c) above? ☐ Yes ☐ No — Amount $ _____

Type _____ @ _____% interest for _____ *years.* Payments/Month = $ _____ *(Principal & Interest only)*

☐ Bank or savings & loan ☐ Fixed rate ☐ New loan

☐ Loan carried by seller ☐ Variable rate ☐ Assumed existing loan balance

Balloon payment ☐ Yes ☐ No Due Date _____ — Amount $ _____

E. WAS AN IMPROVEMENT BOND ASSUMED BY THE BUYER? ☐ Yes ☐ No Outstanding balance: — Amount $ _____

F. TOTAL PURCHASE PRICE (or acquisition price, if traded or exchanged, include real estate commission if paid)

Total Items A through E — $ _____

G. PROPERTY PURCHASED: ☐ Through a broker ☐ Direct from seller ☐ From a family member ☐ Other *(explain)* _____ .

If purchased through a broker, provide broker's name and phone number:

Please explain any special terms, seller concessions, or financing and any other information that would help the Assessor understand the purchase price and terms of sale: _____

_____

PART IV: PROPERTY INFORMATION

A. TYPE OF PROPERTY TRANSFERRED:

☐ Single-family residence ☐ Agricultural ☐ Timeshare

☐ Multiple-family residence (no. of units: _____) ☐ Co-op/Own-your-own ☐ Manufactured home

☐ Commercial/Industrial ☐ Condominium ☐ Unimproved lot

☐ Other (Description: i.e., timber, mineral, water rights, etc. _____)

B. IS THIS PROPERTY INTENDED AS YOUR PRINCIPAL RESIDENCE? ☐ Yes ☐ No

If **yes**, enter the date of occupancy _____ / _____ , 20 _____ or intended occupancy _____ / _____ , 20 _____ .
(month) (day) (month) (day)

C. IS PERSONAL PROPERTY INCLUDED IN THE PURCHASE PRICE (e.g., furniture, farm equipment, machinery, etc.)?

(Other than a manufactured home subject to local property tax?) ☐ Yes ☐ No

If **yes**, enter the value of the personal property included in the purchase price $ _____ *(Attach itemized list of personal property.)*

D. IS A MANUFACTURED HOME INCLUDED IN THE PURCHASE PRICE ☐ Yes ☐ No

If **yes**, how much of the purchase price is allocated to the manufactured home? $ _____ .

Is the manufactured home subject to local property tax? ☐ Yes ☐ No What is the decal number? _____

E. DOES THE PROPERTY PRODUCE INCOME? ☐ Yes ☐ No If **yes**, is the income from:

☐ Lease/Rent ☐ Contract ☐ Mineral Rights ☐ Other—Explain: _____

F. WHAT WAS THE CONDITION OF THE PROPERTY AT THE TIME OF SALE?

☐ Good ☐ Average ☐ Fair ☐ Poor

Please explain the physical condition of the property and provide any other information (such as restrictions, etc.) that would assist the Assessor in determining the value of the property: _____

CERTIFICATION

I certify (or declare) under penalty of perjury under the laws of the State of California that the foregoing and all information hereon, including any accompanying statements or documents, is true, correct, and complete to the best of my knowledge and belief. **This declaration is binding on each and every co-owner and/or partner.**

Signed in County of _____ ,California, this _____ day of _____ 20 _____

SIGNATURE OF OWNER OR CORPORATE OFFICER	TITLE *(if corporate officer/partner)*	E-MAIL ADDRESS *(optional)*

NAME OF NEW OWNER/LEGAL REPRESENTATIVE/CORPORATE OFFICER *(typed or printed)*

The Assessor's Office may contact you for additional information regarding this transaction.

do, the assessor will mail you a form. You don't need to worry about it unless you are sent one.

Many intrafamily transfers of the type discussed in this book do *not* require a Change of Ownership Statement. The discussion of property tax reassessment in Chapter 1 lists types of transfers that are not considered a "change in ownership" and thus do not require a Change of Ownership Statement or property tax reassessment. (Rev. & Tax. Code § 62.)

Like the preliminary form, this form varies slightly from county to county. The information it asks for is similar to that requested on the Preliminary Change of Ownership Report. Again, if you have questions, reread the discussions of title and taxes in Chapters 1 and 3, or ask the clerks in the county recorder's office for help.

You will have 45 days (from the date it's mailed to you) to file the Change of Ownership Statement without penalty. The penalty for late filing is a fine of either $100 or 10% of the taxes on the new assessed property value (up to $2,500), whichever is greater. (Rev. & Tax. Code § 482.)

Step 2: Take the Deed and Tax Statements to the Recorder

After your deed is properly drawn up, signed, and acknowledged (notarized), and the Preliminary Change of Ownership Report has been filled out, the person receiving the property should immediately take (or mail) them to the county recorder's office for the county in which the land is

---

OFFICIAL RECORDS COUNTY OF MARIN

86 59788

RECORDED AT REQUEST OF

Order No.   138565-RH
Escrow No. N-150926-MN
Loan No.

TITLE CO.

1986 OCT 24 AM 8 00

OFFICIAL RECORDS
MARIN COUNTY CALIFORNIA

WHEN RECORDED MAIL TO:

Mr. and Mrs. James Chadwick
495 Oxford Circle
Greenbrae, CA 94904

SPACE ABOVE THIS LINE FOR RECORDER'S USE

MAIL TAX STATEMENTS TO:

DOCUMENTARY TRANSFER TAX $ 240.90
XX
..... Computed on the consideration or value of property conveyed; OR
..... Computed on the consideration or value less liens or encumbrances
remaining at time of sale.

Same as above

_____ FIRST AMERICAN TITLE CO.
Signature of Declarant or Agent determining tax – Firm Name
FIRST AMERICAN TITLE COMPANY

#70-162-02
Tax Code Area 68-004   **GRANT DEED**

FOR A VALUABLE CONSIDERATION, receipt of which is hereby acknowledged,

ROBERT J. TILLSON and WILMA MAE TILLSON, husband and wife

situated. You must take the signed original of the deed for recording.

In many counties, the recorder's office is in the county courthouse. (Two notable exceptions: in Los Angeles it's in the Hall of Records; in San Francisco it's in City Hall.)

If your transaction is subject to the documentary transfer tax, a local tax assessed on property sales, you must pay the tax when the deed is recorded. You should have determined, when you filled out your deed, the amount of tax due. Deeds of trust and some transfer deeds are exempt from the tax.

You will also have to pay a small recording fee. Current fees are about $7 for the first page and $3 for each additional page.

The clerk in the recorder's office will take your original deed, stamp it with the date, time, a filing number, and book and page numbers, make a copy, and give the original back to you. That's it. Filing numbers are given sequentially. The book and page numbers show where the copy of the deed will be found in the county's records, which are now on microfilm in most counties. Recording is effective the minute the clerk accepts your deed.

Recording by mail. Mailing in your deed for recording (with a check for the fees and taxes) is perfectly permissible and can save you lots of time. But before you send off your deed, call the recorder's office and check on fees and documentary transfer taxes.

If you mail the original deed, you should keep at least one photocopy. You should also include a cover letter (a sample letter is shown below) and a stamped, self-addressed envelope so the recorder can return the original of the deed to you. Whether or not you want to trust your deed to the mails is up to you. Certified mail is probably smart, although if you're going to have to stand in line at the post office you may decide it's easier just to go to the recorder's office.

Sample Cover Letter for Recording Deed

James Ferguson
1485 Lafayette St.
Inglewood, CA 98807

February 6, 20xx

County Recorder
227 North Broadway
Los Angeles, CA 90012

Enclosed for recording is a deed transferring real property located at 1230 Lafayette Street, Inglewood, in Los Angeles County. Also enclosed are a Preliminary Change of Ownership Report and a check in the amount of $10.00 to cover the recording fee. As noted on the deed, the transfer is exempt from the documentary transfer tax (Rev. & Tax. Code § 11911).

Please record the deed and return it to me in the enclosed stamped, self-addressed envelope. Thank you.

Sincerely,

James Ferguson

James Ferguson

Time limits. If a deed severing a joint tenancy (see Chapter 2) is executed by only one joint tenant, it must be recorded before that joint tenant's death to defeat the survivorship interests of the remaining joint tenants. The only exception is if the deed is executed fewer than four days before the death of the joint tenant; in that case, it may be recorded up to a week after the death and still terminate the other joint tenants' right of survivorship. (Civ. Code § 683.2.)

There are no other legal time limits for recording. You can record a deed at any time after it's acknowledged, but it obviously makes sense to record it as soon as you can. Delay invites the confusion and trouble that the recording system was set up to avoid.

Recording Checklist

Before you mail or take your deed to the county recorder's office, make sure you have:

- ☐ completely filled out the deed
- ☐ signed the deed and had the signature notarized
- ☐ made a photocopy for each party to the transaction
- ☐ checked the recording fees
- ☐ determined how much, if any, documentary transfer tax you must pay, and
- ☐ filled out a Preliminary Change of Ownership Report.

If you mail the deed, enclose:

- ☐ the original (signed) deed
- ☐ a check for recording fees
- ☐ a check for the documentary transfer tax, if applicable
- ☐ a stamped, self-addressed envelope so the recorder can return the original deed to you, and
- ☐ the Preliminary Change of Ownership Report.

Afterward, be sure to notify the holder of any mortgage of the new owner's name and address, and fill out the Change of Ownership Statement if the assessor sends you one.

 Online recording and tax information. You can find lots of information about recording and real estate taxes online, in many counties. To find your county's website, use this formula:

www.co.[COUNTY NAME].ca.us.

For example, to find the Alameda County site, use:

www.co.Alameda.ca.us.

If that doesn't work, go to Google.com and try this formula:

http://directory.google.com/Top/Regional/
North_America/UnitedStates/California/
Counties[COUNTY NAME].

Chapter 7

When You Need an Expert

Sometimes, whether you're fixing your car, building a deck, or dealing with real estate, you need an expert's help. When it comes to real estate, you may need to consult an accountant, a real estate broker, or one of those pinstriped characters with the briefcases. At several points throughout the book we've suggested that you see an expert if you find yourself in certain situations, including:

- a dispute over ownership of property
- uncertainty about estate planning or federal gift or income tax questions
- an apparent gap in the title to the property
- doubt about the proper way to hold title in your situation, or
- a complicated community property problem.

Where to Go for Help

Many real estate problems don't require the help of an attorney. Before you hire a lawyer, make sure you really have a legal question—not just a question about how things are customarily handled at the county recorder's office or by a title company. Here is how some other experts can help you:

- **Real estate brokers,** who work in the field day in and day out, may have the answer you need at their fingertips. Many are willing to consult with you for a fee, on an hourly basis.
- **Title company employees** and clerks in county recorder's and assessor's offices may be able to assist you with questions about real estate transfers. Often your question may be a simple one that has more to do with local custom than a legal technicality.
- **A tax accountant** is usually the best source of up-to-date information about gift or income taxes. Usually, your best bet is to ask small business owners you know for a recommendation. Once you get a few names, give them a call and outline your problems. Ask what they charge and if they have had experience with your kind of situation.

 • **A lawyer** will probably be needed if there is a dispute over ownership of the property or if you have a serious community property problem. If you decide to see a lawyer, keep in mind that hiring a lawyer does not mean giving up control of whatever task it is that you want to accomplish. You do not have to turn your problem over to a lawyer who will "take care of it" and send you a bill. Your goal should probably be to consult a lawyer on specific questions that come up as you transfer real estate or handle any other routine legal matter yourself. And after reading this book, you should be familiar enough with the concepts and terminology of real estate law to confidently pose your questions.

Accountants

People who have never worked with a certified public account (CPA) who has tax experience are often unsure of how to begin. Many seem to believe that hiring an accountant means calling a huge national accounting firm. In fact, finding a competent local accountant to advise you on tax questions should be easy.

Lawyers

If you do need a lawyer, here are some tips on finding and working with a good one.

Finding a Lawyer

Especially in California, locating a lawyer is no problem. Their advertisements shout from billboards, television, radio, and newspapers, and the Yellow Pages are full of listings. But finding a knowledgeable lawyer who charges reasonable rates, is willing to give you advice in discrete bits, and whom you trust, is not always easy. Picking a name out of the phone book is a common but obviously unreliable method.

*Castles in the air are the only property you
can own without the intervention of lawyers.
Unfortunately, there are no title deeds to them.*
—J. Feidor Rees

Referral panels set up by bar associations are also not high on the list of best ways to find a lawyer. Although lawyers are sometimes listed by specialty, they are rarely screened in any meaningful way. Often the referral panels are just a haven for inexperienced lawyers who need business.

The best way to find a good attorney is to get a recommendation from a friend. People who run small businesses are likely to have consulted a lawyer; ask them who they see and what it costs. They may also know if their attorneys are knowledgeable about real estate law. Attorneys, like everyone else, have become more and more specialized; a lawyer who does personal injury trial work may not have looked at a deed in years.

The lawyer directory at www.nolo.com may be a good resource for you. Lawyers who advertise in the directory describe their areas of practice and answer a series of questions, including whether they are willing to review documents or coach clients who are representing themselves. The directory is new and does not yet cover all of California as this book goes to press, but new lawyers are being added each month, so it's worth a quick check When you get a couple of prospects, call the law offices and outline your problem to the attorney. Explain that you just want to get some questions answered and ask how much an initial consultation will cost. When you find someone you feel comfortable with, make an appointment.

Lawyers' Fees

Lawyers' rates commonly range from about $100 to $350 per hour. It's generally smarter to pay for all consultations with the lawyer, including the first visit, even though some lawyers offer a free short consultation to attract new clients. If you go in for a free initial consultation, you put the lawyer in the position of not making (or even losing) money unless she sells you some services.

If you see an attorney in private practice, one who has a reasonably simple office and lifestyle is more likely to help you for a reasonable cost than is a lawyer who has an elaborate office and a $1,500 suit. (Just remember that the clients paid for the suit.)

Doing Legal Research Yourself

It's always possible to use some of the lawyers' tools without using the lawyers. You can find information on California real estate law online or at any law library. Every county has a law library (in the courthouse), and usually a law librarian will be happy to help you. Law school libraries are also generally open to the public.

A complete guide to legal research, showing you everything from what the books look like to how to research a complicated problem, is *Legal Research: How to Find & Understand the Law,* by Stephen Elias and Susan Levinkind (Nolo).

One of the main resources for real estate problems is the California Civil Code (cited frequently throughout this book), which contains most of the statutes that govern deeds and land transfers. You can get to these statutes easily through Nolo's website, www.nolo.com. Another good way to start is to look under "deeds" in a legal encyclopedia for California called *California Jurisprudence* (usually abbreviated as Cal. Jur.).

Also helpful are publications on real estate that are aimed at lawyers but can be used fairly easily by laypersons. One example is *California Real Estate Law and Practice,* a multivolume reference work published by Matthew Bender Co. The California Department of Real Estate publishes *Real Estate Law,* another helpful book.

Glossary

 Also check out Nolo's free online legal glossary at www.nolo.com.

Acceleration clause. In a promissory note, a clause that allows the lender to declare the entire amount of the loan due if the borrower misses one payment. Due on sale clauses, which make entire real estate loans due if the property is sold, are also referred to as acceleration clauses.

Acknowledgment. A written statement on a deed, made by the person who signs the deed and witnessed by a notary public, that the signature on the deed is valid.

After-acquired title. Title to property that is acquired by someone after that person has purportedly transferred title to it to someone else. Under the law, as soon as the seller actually acquires title, it passes to the person he purported to transfer it to before.

ALTA (American Land Title Association) title insurance policy. A title insurance policy, usually purchased (in the amount of the loan) by a lender financing a real estate purchase, that covers more than the standard (CLTA) policy.

A.P.N. (Assessor's Parcel Number). The designation of property on the local property tax rolls. Some counties require the A.P.N. to be put on deeds that are recorded.

Basis. The figure from which profit on the sale of property is computed for income tax purposes. For example, if your basis in your house is $50,000, and you sell it for $75,000, you make a profit of $25,000. The basis is usually what you paid for the property or its value when you inherited it, subject to certain adjustments for capital improvements and other factors.

Beneficiary. A person who inherits under a will or receives property put in trust. Under a deed of trust that secures a loan, the beneficiary is the lender.

Bequest. A gift made in a will.

Capital improvements. Permanent improvements that increase the value of your property and have a useful life of more than a year—for example, new insulation or a new patio. Ordinary repairs and maintenance don't qualify as capital improvements.

Chain of title. The line of owners of real property, stretching back in time from the current owner to the original grant from some government (in California, often the Spanish government, in the 19th century). An error in this chain of title is what title searches are supposed to find and what title insurance protects you against.

Change of Ownership Statement. A form that asks for information relating to property taxation, which must be filed with the county assessor in certain kinds of real estate transactions. If the form is required, the assessor will send it to the new owner.

CLTA (California Land Title Association) title insurance policy. The standard form for title insurance in

California, usually bought by someone who is buying real property.

Community property. Very generally, all property acquired by a California couple during marriage or registered domestic partnership and before permanent separation, except for gifts to and inheritances by one spouse only. The nature of the property (community or separate) can be changed by written agreement between the couple. See *separate property.*

Community property with right of survivorship. A way of holding title to community property that lets the surviving spouse or domestic partner automatically inherit the property, without probate, when the first one dies.

Conservator. Someone appointed by a court to manage the affairs of a mentally incompetent person.

Consideration. The legal term for something given in exchange for property. Deed forms often say the grantor is transferring property "for good and valuable consideration, receipt of which is hereby acknowledged …." It just means that the grantor got something in exchange for the property.

Corpus. The Latin word for the property held in a trust.

Covenant. A promise. Promises in deeds are usually called covenants.

Covenants, conditions, and restrictions (CC & Rs). Restrictions that govern the use of real property. They are usually enforced by a homeowners' association, and are passed on to the new owners of the property. If your property is subject to CC&Rs, you must tell the buyer this before title is transferred.

Custodian. A person appointed under the Uniform Transfers to Minors Act to manage property for a minor.

Deed. A document that transfers ownership of real property. See *grant, quitclaim,* and *warranty.*

Deed of Trust. See *trust deed.*

Dissolution. The legal term for divorce.

Documentary transfer tax. A tax imposed by cities and counties on sales of real estate. The total charged cannot be more than 55¢ per $500 of the sales price. The tax must be paid before the deed can be recorded.

Domestic partners. See *registered domestic partners.*

Donor. A person who makes a gift.

Due on sale clause. A provision in a mortgage or promissory note that makes the entire amount of a real estate loan due when the property is sold. Also called an *acceleration clause.*

Easement. A legal right to use another's land, usually for a limited purpose. For example, you can grant someone an easement to use a corner of your property as a shortcut to their property. An easement is a legal interest in land, and the written grant of an easement should be recorded. When real property is transferred, a recorded easement goes with it; the new owner takes the property subject to the easement.

Emancipated minor. A minor who has the rights of an adult because he has been married, is in the military, or has been declared emancipated by a court.

Encumbrance. An interest in real property owned by another, such as a lien, mortgage, trust deed, or other claim, which impedes the transfer of title to the land.

Equity. The value of an owner's interest in real property. Calculate equity by subtracting the value of any deeds of trust or other encumbrances from the total value of the property.

Escrow. The process during which a buyer and seller of real estate deposit documents and funds with a third party (the escrow holder, which is usually an escrow or title company) with instructions for making the transfer. To close escrow, the company transfers the buyer's money to the seller and transfers the deed to the property to the buyer.

Fee simple. An old term meaning complete ownership of real property. An owner with a fee simple has no restrictions, inherent in the way he holds title, on his right to transfer the property during his life or leave it by his will. The title may, in reality, have encumbrances that make it harder to transfer; that's another issue.

Fixture. Something that is permanently attached to real property and is considered part of the real property. For example, bookshelves built into a house are fixtures; freestanding bookshelves are considered furniture, not part of the real property. Unless otherwise specified in a sale contract, fixtures are transferred with the real property.

Foreclosure. The forced sale of real property, ordered by a court or under a trustee's power of sale, to pay off a loan that the owner of the property has defaulted on.

Gift tax. Federal tax is imposed when someone gives away valuable property while alive or leaves it at death. A very large amount of property may be given away tax-free; the exact amount depends on the year of death. If any tax is due, it is usually paid only after the person has died.

Grant. The transfer of title to real property by deed or some other document.

Grant deed. A deed that uses the word "grant" and implies certain promises by the grantor about the title to the property. This is the most commonly used kind of deed.

Grantee. The recipient of a grant of real property.

Grantor. The person who signs a deed granting real property to another person or entity. Also, someone who creates a trust.

Heir. A person who inherits property that is not disposed of in a will or trust. A decedent's heirs are determined by statute.

Incumbrance. See *encumbrance*.

Joint tenancy. A way co-owners may hold title to property so that when one co-owner dies, her interest in the property passes directly to the surviving co-owners without probate and regardless of any will provision to the contrary. Compare *tenancy in common*.

Legal description. A description, in a deed, of the location of land, sufficiently detailed to enable a surveyor to identify the property.

Lien. A claim on property for payment of a debt. For example, a tax lien is a lien placed on property when the owner has not paid taxes. A mechanic's lien is imposed by someone who makes improvements on the house (a carpenter, for example). If the carpenter isn't paid, he can enforce his claim by foreclosing on the property. See Civil Code § 3110.

Life estate (life tenancy). An interest in land that is measured by someone's lifetime. The holder of a life estate has the use of the real estate for his lifetime (or, rarely, for the lifetime of someone else) only. When the life estate ends, ownership of the property goes to someone else already chosen by the original owner of the property.

Lis pendens. A notice, recorded in the county recorder's office, of a pending lawsuit that affects title to the land. It gives notice to anyone who is thinking of buying the property that there may be a problem with the current owner's title to the property.

Minor. In California, someone who is less than 18 years old.

Mortgage. A document that makes a piece of real estate security (collateral) for the payment of a debt. If the borrower doesn't pay back the debt on time, the lender can foreclose on the real estate and have it sold to pay off the loan.

Partition. A court-ordered sale or division of jointly owned property. Any co-owner may petition the superior court for a partition order.

Personal property. All possessions that aren't considered real estate (see *real property*).

Power of attorney. Authority to act on another person's behalf. For example, if you will be out of town when your property sale is likely to take place, you can give someone (a co-owner, most likely) the authority to sign the deed for you. A *conventional power of attorney* terminates if the principal becomes incapacitated; a *durable power of attorney* does not.

Preliminary Change of Ownership Report. A form that must be filed with the county recorder whenever real estate changes hands.

Probate. The time-consuming and often expensive process in which a court supervises the transfer of a decedent's estate to heirs and beneficiaries. The necessity for probate can be avoided if property is held in certain forms of ownership, such as joint tenancy, community property, or trusts.

Promissory note. A written promise to pay money.

Property taxes. Local taxes imposed annually on real estate.

Quasi-community property. Property acquired by a married couple while living outside California that would have been community property had the couple been living in California.

Quitclaim deed. A deed that transfers any ownership interest the person signing it may have in particular property but does not guarantee anything about the extent of that interest.

Real Estate Transfer Disclosure Statement. A detailed disclosure form, which a seller is required by law to fill out and give to the buyer before title is transferred. The form covers the condition of the property.

Real property (real estate). Land and things permanently affixed to land, such as buildings.

Reconveyance. The transfer of real estate from a lender to the buyer when a loan secured by the property is paid off.

Recording. The process of filing a copy of a deed with the county recorder for the county in which the land is located. Recording creates a public record of all changes in ownership of all property in the state.

Registered domestic partners. An unmarried couple who have registered as domestic partners with the California Secretary of State.

Remainder. The legal term for the property interest that's left over after someone is given a less than complete interest in land. For example, when someone is given a life estate, the rest of the ownership interest (that is, ownership after the holder of the life estate dies) is called the remainder and must also belong to someone.

Right of survivorship. The right of a surviving owner to take ownership of property held in joint tenancy or as community property with right of survivorship.

Security interest. A claim against property, given by a debtor to ensure payment of a debt. For example, if you borrow money, you may execute a deed of trust on your house, giving the lender the right to have the house sold to pay the debt if you don't pay back the loan. The lender has a security interest in your house.

Separate property. Property that is not community property; that is, property that is acquired by an unmarried person or acquired by gift or inheritance by a married person or registered domestic partner.

Settlor. One who sets up a trust (same as *trustor*).

Special studies zones. Areas of possible earthquake hazards, delineated by state geologists. Sellers must tell buyers if the property is located within a special studies zone.

Tenancy by the entirety. A way for married couples to hold title to property. It is no longer used in California, although some statutes still refer to it.

Tenancy in common. A way for co-owners to hold title that allows them maximum freedom to dispose of their interests by sale, gift, or will. Upon a co-owner's death, his share goes to his beneficiaries (if there is a will) or heirs, not the other co-owners. Compare *joint tenancy*.

Title. Evidence of ownership of real property.

Title company. A company that conducts title searches, issues title insurance, and often handles escrow proceedings.

Title insurance. Insurance that guarantees a buyer against defects in the title of the real property being bought—that is, that no one besides the title holder has any claim to the property.

Title search. A search of the public records in the county recorder's office, usually made by a title insurance company, to see if the current owner of real property actually has good title to the land and that no challenges have been raised.

Trust. A device by which title to property is transferred to a person, called a trustee, who manages the property for the benefit of another person, called a beneficiary. The person who sets up the trust is the trustor or settlor. Trusts can be living (inter vivos), which means set up while the trustor is alive, or testamentary, which means set up in the trustor's will. Living trusts are usually revocable, but they can be made irrevocable.

Trust deed. In California, the most common instrument for financing real estate purchases. The trust deed transfers title to land to a trustee, who holds it as security for a loan. When the loan is paid off, title is transferred to the borrower. The trustee has no powers unless the borrower defaults on the loan or violates one of the other promises in the trust deed; then the trustee can sell the property and pay the lender back from the proceeds.

Trustee. A trustee for a living or testamentary trust manages trust property for a beneficiary. The trustee named in a trust deed does not exercise any control over the property; he has only the power to sell the property if the trust deed is defaulted on.

Trustor. One who sets up a trust (this term has largely been replaced by the term *settlor* or *grantor*). When referring to a deed of trust, the trustor is the borrower—the person who owns the property and signs the deed of trust.

Uniform Transfers to Minors Act. A set of statutes adopted by the California legislature that provides a method for transferring property to minors by allowing the giver to appoint a "custodian" to manage the property for the minor.

Usury. The charging of an illegally high rate of interest on a loan.

Warranty deed. A seldom-used kind of deed, which contains certain express promises about the title being transferred.

■

Appendix

Tear-Out Forms

Grant Deed (2 copies)

Quitclaim Deed (2 copies)

Deed of Trust

Promissory Note Secured by Deed of Trust (2 copies)

Real Estate Transfer Disclosure Statement

Natural Hazard Disclosure Statement

Form for Acknowledgment: Military Personnel

Declaration of Exemption From Documentary Transfer Tax:
    Gift of Real Property

Declaration of Exemption From Documentary Transfer Tax:
    Division of Marital Real Property

Local Option Real Estate Transfer Disclosure Statement

Recording requested by

and when recorded mail
this deed and tax statements to

For recorder's use

Grant Deed

☐ This transfer is exempt from the documentary transfer tax.

☐ The documentary transfer tax is $_____ and is computed on:

    ☐ the full value of the interest or property conveyed.

    ☐ the full value less the value of liens or encumbrances remaining thereon at the time of sale.

The property is located in ☐ an unincorporated area. ☐ the city of _____

For a valuable consideration, receipt of which is hereby acknowledged, _____

_____ hereby grant(s) to _____

_____

the following real property in the City of _____, County of _____ California:

Date: _____   _____

Date: _____   _____

Date: _____   _____

Date: _____   _____

State of California

County of _____ }

On _____, before me, _____,

a notary public in and for said state, personally appeared _____,

personally known to me (or proved to me on the basis of satisfactory evidence) to be the person(s) whose name(s)
is/are subscribed to the within instrument, and acknowledged to me that he/she/they executed the same in his/her/their
authorized capacity(ies) and that by his/her/their signature(s) on the instrument the person(s), or entity upon behalf of
which the person(s) acted, executed the instrument.

_____   [SEAL]

Signature of Notary

Recording requested by

and when recorded mail
this deed and tax statements to

For recorder's use

Grant Deed

☐ This transfer is exempt from the documentary transfer tax.

☐ The documentary transfer tax is $_____ and is computed on:

    ☐ the full value of the interest or property conveyed.

    ☐ the full value less the value of liens or encumbrances remaining thereon at the time of sale.

The property is located in ☐ an unincorporated area. ☐ the city of _____

For a valuable consideration, receipt of which is hereby acknowledged, _____

_____ hereby grant(s) to _____

_____

the following real property in the City of _____, County of _____ California:

Date: _____   _____

Date: _____   _____

Date: _____   _____

Date: _____   _____

State of California

County of _____ }

On _____, before me, _____,

a notary public in and for said state, personally appeared _____

personally known to me (or proved to me on the basis of satisfactory evidence) to be the person(s) whose name(s) is/are subscribed to the within instrument, and acknowledged to me that he/she/they executed the same in his/her/their authorized capacity(ies) and that by his/her/their signature(s) on the instrument the person(s), or entity upon behalf of which the person(s) acted, executed the instrument.

_____   [SEAL]

Signature of Notary

Quitclaim Deed

☐ This transfer is exempt from the documentary transfer tax.

☐ The documentary transfer tax is $_____ and is computed on:

    ☐ the full value of the interest or property conveyed.

    ☐ the full value less the value of liens or encumbrances remaining thereon at the time of sale.

The property is located in ☐ an unincorporated area. ☐ the city of _____

For a valuable consideration, receipt of which is hereby acknowledged, _____

_____ hereby quitclaim(s) to _____

the following real property in the City of _____, County of _____California:

Date: _____   _____

Date: _____   _____

Date: _____   _____

Date: _____   _____

State of California

County of _____ }

On _____, before me, _____,

a notary public in and for said state, personally appeared _____

personally known to me (or proved to me on the basis of satisfactory evidence) to be the person(s) whose name(s) is/are subscribed to the within instrument, and acknowledged to me that he/she/they executed the same in his/her/their authorized capacity(ies) and that by his/her/their signature(s) on the instrument the person(s), or entity upon behalf of which the person(s) acted, executed the instrument.

_____   [SEAL]

Signature of Notary

Recording requested by

and when recorded mail
this deed and tax statements to

For recorder's use

Quitclaim Deed

☐ This transfer is exempt from the documentary transfer tax.

☐ The documentary transfer tax is $_____ and is computed on:

   ☐ the full value of the interest or property conveyed.

   ☐ the full value less the value of liens or encumbrances remaining thereon at the time of sale.

The property is located in ☐ an unincorporated area. ☐ the city of _____

For a valuable consideration, receipt of which is hereby acknowledged, _____

_____ hereby quitclaim(s) to _____

the following real property in the City of _____, County of _____California:

Date: _____   _____

Date: _____   _____

Date: _____   _____

Date: _____   _____

State of California   }

County of _____

On _____, before me, _____,

a notary public in and for said state, personally appeared _____,

personally known to me (or proved to me on the basis of satisfactory evidence) to be the person(s) whose name(s)
is/are subscribed to the within instrument, and acknowledged to me that he/she/they executed the same in his/her/their
authorized capacity(ies) and that by his/her/their signature(s) on the instrument the person(s), or entity upon behalf of
which the person(s) acted, executed the instrument.

_____   [SEAL]

Signature of Notary

After Recording Return To:

_____

_____

_____

_____

_____[Space Above This Line For Recording Data]_____

DEED OF TRUST

DEFINITIONS

Words used in multiple sections of this document are defined below and other words are defined in Sections 3, 11, 13, 18, 20 and 21. Certain rules regarding the usage of words used in this document are also provided in Section 16.

(A)   **"Security Instrument"** means this document, which is dated _____, _____, together with all Riders to this document.

(B) "Borrower" is _____. Borrower is the trustor under this Security Instrument.

(C)   **"Lender"** is _____.   Lender is a _____ organized and existing under the laws of _____. Lender's address is _____ _____. Lender is the beneficiary under this Security Instrument.

(D)   **"Trustee"** is _____.

(E)   **"Note"** means the promissory note signed by Borrower and dated _____, _____. The Note states that Borrower owes Lender _____ _____ Dollars (U.S. $_____) plus interest. Borrower has promised to pay this debt in regular Periodic Payments and to pay the debt in full not later than _____.

(F)   **"Property"** means the property that is described below under the heading "Transfer of Rights in the Property."

(G)   **"Loan"** means the debt evidenced by the Note, plus interest, any prepayment charges and late charges due under the Note, and all sums due under this Security Instrument, plus interest.

(H)   **"Riders"** means all Riders to this Security Instrument that are executed by Borrower. The following Riders are to be executed by Borrower [check box as applicable]:

☐ Adjustable Rate Rider   ☐ Condominium Rider   ☐ Second Home Rider
☐ Balloon Rider   ☐ Planned Unit Development Rider ☐ Other(s) [specify] _____
☐ 1-4 Family Rider   ☐ Biweekly Payment Rider

CALIFORNIA--Single Family--**Fannie Mae/Freddie Mac UNIFORM INSTRUMENT**   Form 3005   1/01   *(page 1 of 16 pages)*

(I) **"Applicable Law"** means all controlling applicable federal, state and local statutes, regulations, ordinances and administrative rules and orders (that have the effect of law) as well as all applicable final, non-appealable judicial opinions.

(J) **"Community Association Dues, Fees, and Assessments"** means all dues, fees, assessments and other charges that are imposed on Borrower or the Property by a condominium association, homeowners association or similar organization.

(K) **"Electronic Funds Transfer"** means any transfer of funds, other than a transaction originated by check, draft, or similar paper instrument, which is initiated through an electronic terminal, telephonic instrument, computer, or magnetic tape so as to order, instruct, or authorize a financial institution to debit or credit an account. Such term includes, but is not limited to, point-of-sale transfers, automated teller machine transactions, transfers initiated by telephone, wire transfers, and automated clearinghouse transfers.

(L) **"Escrow Items"** means those items that are described in Section 3.

(M) **"Miscellaneous Proceeds"** means any compensation, settlement, award of damages, or proceeds paid by any third party (other than insurance proceeds paid under the coverages described in Section 5) for: (i) damage to, or destruction of, the Property; (ii) condemnation or other taking of all or any part of the Property; (iii) conveyance in lieu of condemnation; or (iv) misrepresentations of, or omissions as to, the value and/or condition of the Property.

(N) **"Mortgage Insurance"** means insurance protecting Lender against the nonpayment of, or default on, the Loan.

(O) **"Periodic Payment"** means the regularly scheduled amount due for (i) principal and interest under the Note, plus (ii) any amounts under Section 3 of this Security Instrument.

(P) **"RESPA"** means the Real Estate Settlement Procedures Act (12 U.S.C. §2601 et seq.) and its implementing regulation, Regulation X (24 C.F.R. Part 3500), as they might be amended from time to time, or any additional or successor legislation or regulation that governs the same subject matter. As used in this Security Instrument, "RESPA" refers to all requirements and restrictions that are imposed in regard to a "federally related mortgage loan" even if the Loan does not qualify as a "federally related mortgage loan" under RESPA.

(Q) **"Successor in Interest of Borrower"** means any party that has taken title to the Property, whether or not that party has assumed Borrower's obligations under the Note and/or this Security Instrument.

TRANSFER OF RIGHTS IN THE PROPERTY

This Security Instrument secures to Lender: (i) the repayment of the Loan, and all renewals, extensions and modifications of the Note; and (ii) the performance of Borrower's covenants and agreements under this Security Instrument and the Note. For this purpose, Borrower irrevocably grants and conveys to Trustee, in trust, with power of sale, the following described property located in the _____ of _____:

  [Type of Recording Jurisdiction]   [Name of Recording Jurisdiction] which currently has the address of _____

[Street]

_____, California _____ ("Property Address"):

[City]   [Zip Code]

TOGETHER WITH all the improvements now or hereafter erected on the property, and all easements, appurtenances, and fixtures now or hereafter a part of the property. All replacements and additions shall also be covered by this Security Instrument. All of the foregoing is referred to in this Security Instrument as the "Property."

BORROWER COVENANTS that Borrower is lawfully seised of the estate hereby conveyed and has the right to grant and convey the Property and that the Property is unencumbered, except for encumbrances of record. Borrower warrants and will defend generally the title to the Property against all claims and demands, subject to any encumbrances of record.

THIS SECURITY INSTRUMENT combines uniform covenants for national use and non-uniform covenants with limited variations by jurisdiction to constitute a uniform security instrument covering real property.

UNIFORM COVENANTS. Borrower and Lender covenant and agree as follows:

1. **Payment of Principal, Interest, Escrow Items, Prepayment Charges, and Late Charges.** Borrower shall pay when due the principal of, and interest on, the debt evidenced by the Note and any prepayment charges and late charges due under the Note. Borrower shall also pay funds for Escrow Items pursuant to Section 3. Payments due under the Note and this Security Instrument shall be made in U.S. currency. However, if any check or other instrument received by Lender as payment under the Note or this Security Instrument is returned to Lender unpaid, Lender may require that any or all subsequent payments due under the Note and this Security Instrument be made in one or more of the following forms, as selected by Lender: (a) cash; (b) money order; (c) certified check, bank check, treasurer's check or cashier's check, provided any such check is drawn upon an institution whose deposits are insured by a federal agency, instrumentality, or entity; or (d) Electronic Funds Transfer.

Payments are deemed received by Lender when received at the location designated in the Note or at such other location as may be designated by Lender in accordance with the notice provisions in Section 15. Lender may return any payment or partial payment if the payment or partial payments are insufficient to bring the Loan current. Lender may accept any payment or partial payment insufficient to bring the Loan current, without waiver of any rights hereunder or prejudice to its rights to refuse such payment or partial payments in the future, but Lender is not obligated to apply such payments at the time such payments are accepted. If each Periodic Payment is applied as of its scheduled due date, then Lender need not pay interest on unapplied funds. Lender may hold such unapplied funds until Borrower makes payment to bring the Loan current. If Borrower does not do so within a reasonable period of time, Lender shall either apply such funds or return them to Borrower. If not applied earlier, such funds will be applied to the outstanding principal balance under the Note immediately prior to foreclosure. No offset or claim which Borrower might have now or in the future against Lender shall relieve Borrower from making payments due under the Note and this Security Instrument or performing the covenants and agreements secured by this Security Instrument.

    2.   **Application of Payments or Proceeds.** Except as otherwise described in this Section 2, all payments accepted and applied by Lender shall be applied in the following order of priority: (a) interest due under the Note; (b) principal due under the Note; (c) amounts due under Section 3. Such payments shall be applied to each Periodic Payment in the order in which it became due. Any remaining amounts shall be applied first to late charges, second to any other amounts due under this Security Instrument, and then to reduce the principal balance of the Note.

    If Lender receives a payment from Borrower for a delinquent Periodic Payment which includes a sufficient amount to pay any late charge due, the payment may be applied to the delinquent payment and the late charge. If more than one Periodic Payment is outstanding, Lender may apply any payment received from Borrower to the repayment of the Periodic Payments if, and to the extent that, each payment can be paid in full. To the extent that any excess exists after the payment is applied to the full payment of one or more Periodic Payments, such excess may be applied to any late charges due. Voluntary prepayments shall be applied first to any prepayment charges and then as described in the Note.

    Any application of payments, insurance proceeds, or Miscellaneous Proceeds to principal due under the Note shall not extend or postpone the due date, or change the amount, of the Periodic Payments.

    3.   **Funds for Escrow Items.** Borrower shall pay to Lender on the day Periodic Payments are due under the Note, until the Note is paid in full, a sum (the "Funds") to provide for payment of amounts due for: (a) taxes and assessments and other items which can attain priority over this Security Instrument as a lien or encumbrance on the Property; (b) leasehold payments or ground rents on the Property, if any; (c) premiums for any and all insurance required by Lender under Section 5; and (d) Mortgage Insurance premiums, if any, or any sums payable by Borrower to Lender in lieu of the payment of Mortgage Insurance premiums in accordance with the provisions of Section 10. These items are called "Escrow Items." At origination or at any time during the term of the Loan, Lender may require that Community Association Dues, Fees, and Assessments, if any, be escrowed by Borrower, and such dues, fees and assessments shall be an Escrow Item. Borrower shall promptly furnish to Lender all notices of amounts to be paid under this Section. Borrower shall pay Lender the Funds for Escrow Items unless Lender waives Borrower's obligation to pay the Funds for any or all Escrow Items. Lender may waive Borrower's obligation to pay to Lender Funds for any or all Escrow Items at any time. Any such waiver may only be in writing. In the event of such waiver, Borrower shall pay directly, when and where payable, the amounts due for any Escrow Items for which payment of Funds has been waived by Lender and, if Lender requires, shall furnish to Lender receipts evidencing such payment within such time period as Lender may require. Borrower's obligation to make such payments and to provide receipts shall for all purposes be deemed to be a covenant and agreement contained in this Security Instrument, as the phrase "covenant and agreement" is used in Section 9. If Borrower is obligated to pay Escrow Items directly, pursuant to a waiver, and Borrower fails to pay the amount due for an Escrow Item, Lender may exercise its rights under Section 9 and pay such amount and Borrower shall then be obligated under Section 9 to repay to Lender any such amount. Lender may revoke the waiver as to any or all Escrow Items at any time by a notice given in accordance with Section 15 and, upon such revocation, Borrower shall pay to Lender all Funds, and in such amounts, that are then required under this Section 3.

Lender may, at any time, collect and hold Funds in an amount (a) sufficient to permit Lender to apply the Funds at the time specified under RESPA, and (b) not to exceed the maximum amount a lender can require under RESPA. Lender shall estimate the amount of Funds due on the basis of current data and reasonable estimates of expenditures of future Escrow Items or otherwise in accordance with Applicable Law.

The Funds shall be held in an institution whose deposits are insured by a federal agency, instrumentality, or entity (including Lender, if Lender is an institution whose deposits are so insured) or in any Federal Home Loan Bank. Lender shall apply the Funds to pay the Escrow Items no later than the time specified under RESPA. Lender shall not charge Borrower for holding and applying the Funds, annually analyzing the escrow account, or verifying the Escrow Items, unless Lender pays Borrower interest on the Funds and Applicable Law permits Lender to make such a charge. Unless an agreement is made in writing or Applicable Law requires interest to be paid on the Funds, Lender shall not be required to pay Borrower any interest or earnings on the Funds. Borrower and Lender can agree in writing, however, that interest shall be paid on the Funds. Lender shall give to Borrower, without charge, an annual accounting of the Funds as required by RESPA.

If there is a surplus of Funds held in escrow, as defined under RESPA, Lender shall account to Borrower for the excess funds in accordance with RESPA. If there is a shortage of Funds held in escrow, as defined under RESPA, Lender shall notify Borrower as required by RESPA, and Borrower shall pay to Lender the amount necessary to make up the shortage in accordance with RESPA, but in no more than 12 monthly payments. If there is a deficiency of Funds held in escrow, as defined under RESPA, Lender shall notify Borrower as required by RESPA, and Borrower shall pay to Lender the amount necessary to make up the deficiency in accordance with RESPA, but in no more than 12 monthly payments.

Upon payment in full of all sums secured by this Security Instrument, Lender shall promptly refund to Borrower any Funds held by Lender.

4. **Charges; Liens.** Borrower shall pay all taxes, assessments, charges, fines, and impositions attributable to the Property which can attain priority over this Security Instrument, leasehold payments or ground rents on the Property, if any, and Community Association Dues, Fees, and Assessments, if any. To the extent that these items are Escrow Items, Borrower shall pay them in the manner provided in Section 3.

Borrower shall promptly discharge any lien which has priority over this Security Instrument unless Borrower: (a) agrees in writing to the payment of the obligation secured by the lien in a manner acceptable to Lender, but only so long as Borrower is performing such agreement; (b) contests the lien in good faith by, or defends against enforcement of the lien in, legal proceedings which in Lender's opinion operate to prevent the enforcement of the lien while those proceedings are pending, but only until such proceedings are concluded; or (c) secures from the holder of the lien an agreement satisfactory to Lender subordinating the lien to this Security Instrument. If Lender determines that any part of the Property is subject to a lien which can attain priority over this Security Instrument, Lender may give Borrower a notice identifying the lien. Within 10 days of the date on which that notice is given, Borrower shall satisfy the lien or take one or more of the actions set forth above in this Section 4.

Lender may require Borrower to pay a one-time charge for a real estate tax verification and/or reporting service used by Lender in connection with this Loan.

5.   Property Insurance. Borrower shall keep the improvements now existing or hereafter erected on the Property insured against loss by fire, hazards included within the term "extended coverage," and any other hazards including, but not limited to, earthquakes and floods, for which Lender requires insurance. This insurance shall be maintained in the amounts (including deductible levels) and for the periods that Lender requires. What Lender requires pursuant to the preceding sentences can change during the term of the Loan. The insurance carrier providing the insurance shall be chosen by Borrower subject to Lender's right to disapprove Borrower's choice, which right shall not be exercised unreasonably. Lender may require Borrower to pay, in connection with this Loan, either: (a) a one-time charge for flood zone determination, certification and tracking services; or (b) a one-time charge for flood zone determination and certification services and subsequent charges each time remappings or similar changes occur which reasonably might affect such determination or certification. Borrower shall also be responsible for the payment of any fees imposed by the Federal Emergency Management Agency in connection with the review of any flood zone determination resulting from an objection by Borrower.

If Borrower fails to maintain any of the coverages described above, Lender may obtain insurance coverage, at Lender's option and Borrower's expense. Lender is under no obligation to purchase any particular type or amount of coverage. Therefore, such coverage shall cover Lender, but might or might not protect Borrower, Borrower's equity in the Property, or the contents of the Property, against any risk, hazard or liability and might provide greater or lesser coverage than was previously in effect. Borrower acknowledges that the cost of the insurance coverage so obtained might significantly exceed the cost of insurance that Borrower could have obtained. Any amounts disbursed by Lender under this Section 5 shall become additional debt of Borrower secured by this Security Instrument. These amounts shall bear interest at the Note rate from the date of disbursement and shall be payable, with such interest, upon notice from Lender to Borrower requesting payment.

All insurance policies required by Lender and renewals of such policies shall be subject to Lender's right to disapprove such policies, shall include a standard mortgage clause, and shall name Lender as mortgagee and/or as an additional loss payee and Borrower further agrees to generally assign rights to insurance proceeds to the holder of the Note up to the amount of the outstanding loan balance. Lender shall have the right to hold the policies and renewal certificates. If Lender requires, Borrower shall promptly give to Lender all receipts of paid premiums and renewal notices. If Borrower obtains any form of insurance coverage, not otherwise required by Lender, for damage to, or destruction of, the Property, such policy shall include a standard mortgage clause and shall name Lender as mortgagee and/or as an additional loss payee and Borrower further agrees to generally assign rights to insurance proceeds to the holder of the Note up to the amount of the outstanding loan balance.

In the event of loss, Borrower shall give prompt notice to the insurance carrier and Lender. Lender may make proof of loss if not made promptly by Borrower. Unless Lender and Borrower otherwise agree in writing, any insurance proceeds, whether or not the underlying insurance was required by Lender, shall be applied to restoration or repair of the Property, if the restoration or repair is economically feasible and Lender's security is not lessened. During such repair and restoration period, Lender shall have the right to hold such insurance proceeds until Lender has had an opportunity to inspect such Property to ensure the work has been completed to Lender's satisfaction, provided that such inspection shall be undertaken promptly. Lender may disburse proceeds for the repairs and restoration in a single payment or in a series of progress payments as the work is completed. Unless an agreement is made in writing or Applicable Law requires interest to be paid on such insurance proceeds, Lender shall not be required to pay Borrower any interest or earnings on such proceeds. Fees for public adjusters, or other third parties, retained by Borrower shall not be paid out of the insurance proceeds and shall be the sole obligation of Borrower. If the restoration or repair is not economically feasible or Lender's security would be lessened, the insurance proceeds shall be applied to the sums secured by this Security Instrument, whether or not then due, with the excess, if any, paid to Borrower. Such insurance proceeds shall be applied in the order provided for in Section 2.

If Borrower abandons the Property, Lender may file, negotiate and settle any available insurance claim and related matters. If Borrower does not respond within 30 days to a notice from Lender that the insurance carrier has offered to settle a claim, then Lender may negotiate and settle the claim. The 30-day period will begin when the notice is given. In either event, or if Lender acquires the Property under Section 22 or otherwise, Borrower hereby assigns to Lender (a) Borrower's rights to any insurance proceeds in an amount not to exceed the amounts unpaid under the Note or this Security Instrument, and (b) any other of Borrower's rights (other than the right to any refund of unearned premiums paid by Borrower) under all insurance policies covering the Property, insofar as such rights are applicable to the coverage of the Property. Lender may use the insurance proceeds either to repair or restore the Property or to pay amounts unpaid under the Note or this Security Instrument, whether or not then due.

6. **Occupancy.** Borrower shall occupy, establish, and use the Property as Borrower's principal residence within 60 days after the execution of this Security Instrument and shall continue to occupy the Property as Borrower's principal residence for at least one year after the date of occupancy, unless Lender otherwise agrees in writing, which consent shall not be unreasonably withheld, or unless extenuating circumstances exist which are beyond Borrower's control.

7. **Preservation, Maintenance and Protection of the Property; Inspections.** Borrower shall not destroy, damage or impair the Property, allow the Property to deteriorate or commit waste on the Property. Whether or not Borrower is residing in the Property, Borrower shall maintain the Property in order to prevent the Property from deteriorating or decreasing in value due to its condition. Unless it is determined pursuant to Section 5 that repair or restoration is not economically feasible, Borrower shall promptly repair the Property if damaged to avoid further deterioration or damage. If insurance or condemnation proceeds are paid in connection with damage to, or the taking of, the Property, Borrower shall be responsible for repairing or restoring the Property only if Lender has released proceeds for such purposes. Lender may disburse proceeds for the repairs and restoration in a single payment or in a series of progress payments as the work is completed. If the insurance or condemnation proceeds are not sufficient to repair or restore the Property, Borrower is not relieved of Borrower's obligation for the completion of such repair or restoration.

Lender or its agent may make reasonable entries upon and inspections of the Property. If it has reasonable cause, Lender may inspect the interior of the improvements on the Property. Lender shall give Borrower notice at the time of or prior to such an interior inspection specifying such reasonable cause.

8. **Borrower's Loan Application.** Borrower shall be in default if, during the Loan application process, Borrower or any persons or entities acting at the direction of Borrower or with Borrower's knowledge or consent gave materially false, misleading, or inaccurate information or statements to Lender (or failed to provide Lender with material information) in

connection with the Loan. Material representations include, but are not limited to, representations concerning Borrower's occupancy of the Property as Borrower's principal residence.

   9.   **Protection of Lender's Interest in the Property and Rights Under this Security Instrument.** If (a) Borrower fails to perform the covenants and agreements contained in this Security Instrument, (b) there is a legal proceeding that might significantly affect Lender's interest in the Property and/or rights under this Security Instrument (such as a proceeding in bankruptcy, probate, for condemnation or forfeiture, for enforcement of a lien which may attain priority over this Security Instrument or to enforce laws or regulations), or (c) Borrower has abandoned the Property, then Lender may do and pay for whatever is reasonable or appropriate to protect Lender's interest in the Property and rights under this Security Instrument, including protecting and/or assessing the value of the Property, and securing and/or repairing the Property. Lender's actions can include, but are not limited to: (a) paying any sums secured by a lien which has priority over this Security Instrument; (b) appearing in court; and (c) paying reasonable attorneys' fees to protect its interest in the Property and/or rights under this Security Instrument, including its secured position in a bankruptcy proceeding. Securing the Property includes, but is not limited to, entering the Property to make repairs, change locks, replace or board up doors and windows, drain water from pipes, eliminate building or other code violations or dangerous conditions, and have utilities turned on or off. Although Lender may take action under this Section 9, Lender does not have to do so and is not under any duty or obligation to do so. It is agreed that Lender incurs no liability for not taking any or all actions authorized under this Section 9.

   Any amounts disbursed by Lender under this Section 9 shall become additional debt of Borrower secured by this Security Instrument. These amounts shall bear interest at the Note rate from the date of disbursement and shall be payable, with such interest, upon notice from Lender to Borrower requesting payment.

   If this Security Instrument is on a leasehold, Borrower shall comply with all the provisions of the lease. If Borrower acquires fee title to the Property, the leasehold and the fee title shall not merge unless Lender agrees to the merger in writing.

   10.   **Mortgage Insurance.** If Lender required Mortgage Insurance as a condition of making the Loan, Borrower shall pay the premiums required to maintain the Mortgage Insurance in effect. If, for any reason, the Mortgage Insurance coverage required by Lender ceases to be available from the mortgage insurer that previously provided such insurance and Borrower was required to make separately designated payments toward the premiums for Mortgage Insurance, Borrower shall pay the premiums required to obtain coverage substantially equivalent to the Mortgage Insurance previously in effect, at a cost substantially equivalent to the cost to Borrower of the Mortgage Insurance previously in effect, from an alternate mortgage insurer selected by Lender. If substantially equivalent Mortgage Insurance coverage is not available, Borrower shall continue to pay to Lender the amount of the separately designated payments that were due when the insurance coverage ceased to be in effect. Lender will accept, use and retain these payments as a non-refundable loss reserve in lieu of Mortgage Insurance. Such loss reserve shall be non-refundable, notwithstanding the fact that the Loan is ultimately paid in full, and Lender shall not be required to pay Borrower any interest or earnings on such loss reserve. Lender can no longer require loss reserve payments if Mortgage Insurance coverage (in the amount and for the period that Lender requires) provided by an insurer selected by Lender again becomes available, is obtained, and Lender requires separately designated payments toward the

premiums for Mortgage Insurance. If Lender required Mortgage Insurance as a condition of making the Loan and Borrower was required to make separately designated payments toward the premiums for Mortgage Insurance, Borrower shall pay the premiums required to maintain Mortgage Insurance in effect, or to provide a non-refundable loss reserve, until Lender's requirement for Mortgage Insurance ends in accordance with any written agreement between Borrower and Lender providing for such termination or until termination is required by Applicable Law. Nothing in this Section 10 affects Borrower's obligation to pay interest at the rate provided in the Note.

Mortgage Insurance reimburses Lender (or any entity that purchases the Note) for certain losses it may incur if Borrower does not repay the Loan as agreed. Borrower is not a party to the Mortgage Insurance.

Mortgage insurers evaluate their total risk on all such insurance in force from time to time, and may enter into agreements with other parties that share or modify their risk, or reduce losses. These agreements are on terms and conditions that are satisfactory to the mortgage insurer and the other party (or parties) to these agreements. These agreements may require the mortgage insurer to make payments using any source of funds that the mortgage insurer may have available (which may include funds obtained from Mortgage Insurance premiums).

As a result of these agreements, Lender, any purchaser of the Note, another insurer, any reinsurer, any other entity, or any affiliate of any of the foregoing, may receive (directly or indirectly) amounts that derive from (or might be characterized as) a portion of Borrower's payments for Mortgage Insurance, in exchange for sharing or modifying the mortgage insurer's risk, or reducing losses. If such agreement provides that an affiliate of Lender takes a share of the insurer's risk in exchange for a share of the premiums paid to the insurer, the arrangement is often termed "captive reinsurance." Further:

(a)   Any such agreements will not affect the amounts that Borrower has agreed to pay for Mortgage Insurance, or any other terms of the Loan. Such agreements will not increase the amount Borrower will owe for Mortgage Insurance, and they will not entitle Borrower to any refund.

(b)   Any such agreements will not affect the rights Borrower has - if any - with respect to the Mortgage Insurance under the Homeowners Protection Act of 1998 or any other law. These rights may include the right to receive certain disclosures, to request and obtain cancellation of the Mortgage Insurance, to have the Mortgage Insurance terminated automatically, and/or to receive a refund of any Mortgage Insurance premiums that were unearned at the time of such cancellation or termination.

11.   **Assignment of Miscellaneous Proceeds; Forfeiture.**   All Miscellaneous Proceeds are hereby assigned to and shall be paid to Lender.

If the Property is damaged, such Miscellaneous Proceeds shall be applied to restoration or repair of the Property, if the restoration or repair is economically feasible and Lender's security is not lessened. During such repair and restoration period, Lender shall have the right to hold such Miscellaneous Proceeds until Lender has had an opportunity to inspect such Property to ensure the work has been completed to Lender's satisfaction, provided that such inspection shall be undertaken promptly. Lender may pay for the repairs and restoration in a single disbursement or in a series of progress payments as the work is completed. Unless an agreement is made in writing or Applicable Law requires interest to be paid on such Miscellaneous Proceeds, Lender shall not be required to pay Borrower any interest or earnings on such Miscellaneous Proceeds. If the restoration or repair is not economically feasible or Lender's security would be lessened, the Miscellaneous Proceeds shall be applied to the sums secured by this Security Instrument, whether or not then due, with the excess, if any, paid to Borrower. Such Miscellaneous Proceeds shall be applied in the order provided for in Section 2.

In the event of a total taking, destruction, or loss in value of the Property, the Miscellaneous Proceeds shall be applied to the sums secured by this Security Instrument, whether or not then due, with the excess, if any, paid to Borrower.

In the event of a partial taking, destruction, or loss in value of the Property in which the fair market value of the Property immediately before the partial taking, destruction, or loss in value is equal to or greater than the amount of the sums secured by this Security Instrument immediately before the partial taking, destruction, or loss in value, unless Borrower and Lender otherwise agree in writing, the sums secured by this Security Instrument shall be reduced by the amount of the Miscellaneous Proceeds multiplied by the following fraction: (a) the total amount of the sums secured immediately before the partial taking, destruction, or loss in value divided by (b) the fair market value of the Property immediately before the partial taking, destruction, or loss in value. Any balance shall be paid to Borrower.

In the event of a partial taking, destruction, or loss in value of the Property in which the fair market value of the Property immediately before the partial taking, destruction, or loss in value is less than the amount of the sums secured immediately before the partial taking, destruction, or loss in value, unless Borrower and Lender otherwise agree in writing, the Miscellaneous Proceeds shall be applied to the sums secured by this Security Instrument whether or not the sums are then due.

If the Property is abandoned by Borrower, or if, after notice by Lender to Borrower that the Opposing Party (as defined in the next sentence) offers to make an award to settle a claim for damages, Borrower fails to respond to Lender within 30 days after the date the notice is given, Lender is authorized to collect and apply the Miscellaneous Proceeds either to restoration or repair of the Property or to the sums secured by this Security Instrument, whether or not then due. "Opposing Party" means the third party that owes Borrower Miscellaneous Proceeds or the party against whom Borrower has a right of action in regard to Miscellaneous Proceeds.

Borrower shall be in default if any action or proceeding, whether civil or criminal, is begun that, in Lender's judgment, could result in forfeiture of the Property or other material impairment of Lender's interest in the Property or rights under this Security Instrument. Borrower can cure such a default and, if acceleration has occurred, reinstate as provided in Section 19, by causing the action or proceeding to be dismissed with a ruling that, in Lender's judgment, precludes forfeiture of the Property or other material impairment of Lender's interest in the Property or rights under this Security Instrument. The proceeds of any award or claim for damages that are attributable to the impairment of Lender's interest in the Property are hereby assigned and shall be paid to Lender.

All Miscellaneous Proceeds that are not applied to restoration or repair of the Property shall be applied in the order provided for in Section 2.

12. **Borrower Not Released; Forbearance By Lender Not a Waiver.** Extension of the time for payment or modification of amortization of the sums secured by this Security Instrument granted by Lender to Borrower or any Successor in Interest of Borrower shall not operate to release the liability of Borrower or any Successors in Interest of Borrower. Lender shall not be required to commence proceedings against any Successor in Interest of Borrower or to refuse to extend time for payment or otherwise modify amortization of the sums secured by this Security Instrument by reason of any demand made by the original Borrower or any

Successors in Interest of Borrower. Any forbearance by Lender in exercising any right or remedy including, without limitation, Lender's acceptance of payments from third persons, entities or Successors in Interest of Borrower or in amounts less than the amount then due, shall not be a waiver of or preclude the exercise of any right or remedy.

     13.   **Joint and Several Liability; Co-signers; Successors and Assigns Bound.** Borrower covenants and agrees that Borrower's obligations and liability shall be joint and several. However, any Borrower who co-signs this Security Instrument but does not execute the Note (a "co-signer"): (a) is co-signing this Security Instrument only to mortgage, grant and convey the co-signer's interest in the Property under the terms of this Security Instrument; (b) is not personally obligated to pay the sums secured by this Security Instrument; and (c) agrees that Lender and any other Borrower can agree to extend, modify, forbear or make any accommodations with regard to the terms of this Security Instrument or the Note without the co-signer's consent.

     Subject to the provisions of Section 18, any Successor in Interest of Borrower who assumes Borrower's obligations under this Security Instrument in writing, and is approved by Lender, shall obtain all of Borrower's rights and benefits under this Security Instrument. Borrower shall not be released from Borrower's obligations and liability under this Security Instrument unless Lender agrees to such release in writing. The covenants and agreements of this Security Instrument shall bind (except as provided in Section 20) and benefit the successors and assigns of Lender.

     14.   **Loan Charges.** Lender may charge Borrower fees for services performed in connection with Borrower's default, for the purpose of protecting Lender's interest in the Property and rights under this Security Instrument, including, but not limited to, attorneys' fees, property inspection and valuation fees. In regard to any other fees, the absence of express authority in this Security Instrument to charge a specific fee to Borrower shall not be construed as a prohibition on the charging of such fee. Lender may not charge fees that are expressly prohibited by this Security Instrument or by Applicable Law.

     If the Loan is subject to a law which sets maximum loan charges, and that law is finally interpreted so that the interest or other loan charges collected or to be collected in connection with the Loan exceed the permitted limits, then: (a) any such loan charge shall be reduced by the amount necessary to reduce the charge to the permitted limit; and (b) any sums already collected from Borrower which exceeded permitted limits will be refunded to Borrower. Lender may choose to make this refund by reducing the principal owed under the Note or by making a direct payment to Borrower. If a refund reduces principal, the reduction will be treated as a partial prepayment without any prepayment charge (whether or not a prepayment charge is provided for under the Note). Borrower's acceptance of any such refund made by direct payment to Borrower will constitute a waiver of any right of action Borrower might have arising out of such overcharge.

     15.   **Notices.** All notices given by Borrower or Lender in connection with this Security Instrument must be in writing. Any notice to Borrower in connection with this Security Instrument shall be deemed to have been given to Borrower when mailed by first class mail or when actually delivered to Borrower's notice address if sent by other means. Notice to any one Borrower shall constitute notice to all Borrowers unless Applicable Law expressly requires otherwise. The notice address shall be the Property Address unless Borrower has designated a substitute notice address by notice to Lender. Borrower shall promptly notify Lender of Borrower's change of address. If Lender specifies a procedure for reporting Borrower's change of address, then Borrower shall only report a change of address through that specified procedure. There may be only one designated notice address under this Security Instrument at any one time. Any notice to Lender shall be given by delivering it or by mailing it by first class mail to Lender's address stated herein unless Lender has designated another address by notice to Borrower. Any notice in connection with this Security Instrument shall not be deemed to have been given to Lender until actually received by Lender. If any notice required by this Security Instrument is also required under Applicable Law, the Applicable Law requirement will satisfy the corresponding requirement under this Security Instrument.

16.   Governing Law; Severability; Rules of Construction.   This Security Instrument shall be governed by federal law and the law of the jurisdiction in which the Property is located. All rights and obligations contained in this Security Instrument are subject to any requirements and limitations of Applicable Law. Applicable Law might explicitly or implicitly allow the parties to agree by contract or it might be silent, but such silence shall not be construed as a prohibition against agreement by contract. In the event that any provision or clause of this Security Instrument or the Note conflicts with Applicable Law, such conflict shall not affect other provisions of this Security Instrument or the Note which can be given effect without the conflicting provision.

As used in this Security Instrument: (a) words of the masculine gender shall mean and include corresponding neuter words or words of the feminine gender; (b) words in the singular shall mean and include the plural and vice versa; and (c) the word "may" gives sole discretion without any obligation to take any action.

17.   Borrower's Copy.   Borrower shall be given one copy of the Note and of this Security Instrument.

18.   Transfer of the Property or a Beneficial Interest in Borrower.   As used in this Section 18, "Interest in the Property" means any legal or beneficial interest in the Property, including, but not limited to, those beneficial interests transferred in a bond for deed, contract for deed, installment sales contract or escrow agreement, the intent of which is the transfer of title by Borrower at a future date to a purchaser.

If all or any part of the Property or any Interest in the Property is sold or transferred (or if Borrower is not a natural person and a beneficial interest in Borrower is sold or transferred) without Lender's prior written consent, Lender may require immediate payment in full of all sums secured by this Security Instrument. However, this option shall not be exercised by Lender if such exercise is prohibited by Applicable Law.

If Lender exercises this option, Lender shall give Borrower notice of acceleration. The notice shall provide a period of not less than 30 days from the date the notice is given in accordance with Section 15 within which Borrower must pay all sums secured by this Security Instrument. If Borrower fails to pay these sums prior to the expiration of this period, Lender may invoke any remedies permitted by this Security Instrument without further notice or demand on Borrower.

19.   Borrower's Right to Reinstate After Acceleration.   If Borrower meets certain conditions, Borrower shall have the right to have enforcement of this Security Instrument discontinued at any time prior to the earliest of: (a) five days before sale of the Property pursuant to any power of sale contained in this Security Instrument; (b) such other period as Applicable Law might specify for the termination of Borrower's right to reinstate; or (c) entry of a judgment enforcing this Security Instrument. Those conditions are that Borrower: (a) pays Lender all sums which then would be due under this Security Instrument and the Note as if no acceleration had occurred; (b) cures any default of any other covenants or agreements; (c) pays all expenses incurred in enforcing this Security Instrument, including, but not limited to, reasonable attorneys' fees, property inspection and valuation fees, and other fees incurred for the purpose of protecting Lender's interest in the Property and rights under this Security Instrument; and (d) takes such action as Lender may reasonably require to assure that Lender's interest in the Property and rights under this Security Instrument, and Borrower's obligation to pay the sums secured by this Security Instrument, shall continue unchanged. Lender may require that Borrower pay such reinstatement sums and expenses in one or more of the following forms, as selected by Lender: (a) cash; (b) money order; (c) certified check, bank check, treasurer's check or cashier's check, provided any such check is drawn upon an institution whose deposits are insured by a federal agency, instrumentality or entity; or (d) Electronic Funds Transfer. Upon reinstatement by Borrower, this Security Instrument and obligations secured hereby shall remain fully effective as if no acceleration had occurred. However, this right to reinstate shall not apply in the case of acceleration under Section 18.

     20.   Sale of Note; Change of Loan Servicer; Notice of Grievance. The Note or a partial interest in the Note (together with this Security Instrument) can be sold one or more times without prior notice to Borrower. A sale might result in a change in the entity (known as the "Loan Servicer") that collects Periodic Payments due under the Note and this Security Instrument and performs other mortgage loan servicing obligations under the Note, this Security Instrument, and Applicable Law. There also might be one or more changes of the Loan Servicer unrelated to a sale of the Note. If there is a change of the Loan Servicer, Borrower will be given written notice of the change which will state the name and address of the new Loan Servicer, the address to which payments should be made and any other information RESPA requires in connection with a notice of transfer of servicing. If the Note is sold and thereafter the Loan is serviced by a Loan Servicer other than the purchaser of the Note, the mortgage loan servicing obligations to Borrower will remain with the Loan Servicer or be transferred to a successor Loan Servicer and are not assumed by the Note purchaser unless otherwise provided by the Note purchaser.

     Neither Borrower nor Lender may commence, join, or be joined to any judicial action (as either an individual litigant or the member of a class) that arises from the other party's actions pursuant to this Security Instrument or that alleges that the other party has breached any provision of, or any duty owed by reason of, this Security Instrument, until such Borrower or Lender has notified the other party (with such notice given in compliance with the requirements of Section 15) of such alleged breach and afforded the other party hereto a reasonable period after the giving of such notice to take corrective action. If Applicable Law provides a time period which must elapse before certain action can be taken, that time period will be deemed to be reasonable for purposes of this paragraph. The notice of acceleration and opportunity to cure given to Borrower pursuant to Section 22 and the notice of acceleration given to Borrower pursuant to Section 18 shall be deemed to satisfy the notice and opportunity to take corrective action provisions of this Section 20.

     21.   Hazardous Substances. As used in this Section 21: (a) "Hazardous Substances" are those substances defined as toxic or hazardous substances, pollutants, or wastes by Environmental Law and the following substances: gasoline, kerosene, other flammable or toxic petroleum products, toxic pesticides and herbicides, volatile solvents, materials containing asbestos or formaldehyde, and radioactive materials; (b) "Environmental Law" means federal laws and laws of the jurisdiction where the Property is located that relate to health, safety or environmental protection; (c) "Environmental Cleanup" includes any response action, remedial action, or removal action, as defined in Environmental Law; and (d) an "Environmental Condition" means a condition that can cause, contribute to, or otherwise trigger an Environmental Cleanup.

Borrower shall not cause or permit the presence, use, disposal, storage, or release of any Hazardous Substances, or threaten to release any Hazardous Substances, on or in the Property. Borrower shall not do, nor allow anyone else to do, anything affecting the Property (a) that is in violation of any Environmental Law, (b) which creates an Environmental Condition, or (c) which, due to the presence, use, or release of a Hazardous Substance, creates a condition that adversely affects the value of the Property. The preceding two sentences shall not apply to the presence, use, or storage on the Property of small quantities of Hazardous Substances that are generally recognized to be appropriate to normal residential uses and to maintenance of the Property (including, but not limited to, hazardous substances in consumer products).

Borrower shall promptly give Lender written notice of (a) any investigation, claim, demand, lawsuit or other action by any governmental or regulatory agency or private party involving the Property and any Hazardous Substance or Environmental Law of which Borrower has actual knowledge, (b) any Environmental Condition, including but not limited to, any spilling, leaking, discharge, release or threat of release of any Hazardous Substance, and (c) any condition caused by the presence, use or release of a Hazardous Substance which adversely affects the value of the Property. If Borrower learns, or is notified by any governmental or regulatory authority, or any private party, that any removal or other remediation of any Hazardous Substance affecting the Property is necessary, Borrower shall promptly take all necessary remedial actions in accordance with Environmental Law. Nothing herein shall create any obligation on Lender for an Environmental Cleanup.

NON-UNIFORM COVENANTS. Borrower and Lender further covenant and agree as follows:

22. Acceleration; Remedies. Lender shall give notice to Borrower prior to acceleration following Borrower's breach of any covenant or agreement in this Security Instrument (but not prior to acceleration under Section 18 unless Applicable Law provides otherwise). The notice shall specify: (a) the default; (b) the action required to cure the default; (c) a date, not less than 30 days from the date the notice is given to Borrower, by which the default must be cured; and (d) that failure to cure the default on or before the date specified in the notice may result in acceleration of the sums secured by this Security Instrument and sale of the Property. The notice shall further inform Borrower of the right to reinstate after acceleration and the right to bring a court action to assert the non-existence of a default or any other defense of Borrower to acceleration and sale. If the default is not cured on or before the date specified in the notice, Lender at its option may require immediate payment in full of all sums secured by this Security Instrument without further demand and may invoke the power of sale and any other remedies permitted by Applicable Law. Lender shall be entitled to collect all expenses incurred in pursuing the remedies provided in this Section 22, including, but not limited to, reasonable attorneys' fees and costs of title evidence.

If Lender invokes the power of sale, Lender shall execute or cause Trustee to execute a written notice of the occurrence of an event of default and of Lender's election to cause the Property to be sold. Trustee shall cause this notice to be recorded in each county

in which any part of the Property is located. Lender or Trustee shall mail copies of the notice as prescribed by Applicable Law to Borrower and to the other persons prescribed by Applicable Law. Trustee shall give public notice of sale to the persons and in the manner prescribed by Applicable Law. After the time required by Applicable Law, Trustee, without demand on Borrower, shall sell the Property at public auction to the highest bidder at the time and place and under the terms designated in the notice of sale in one or more parcels and in any order Trustee determines. Trustee may postpone sale of all or any parcel of the Property by public announcement at the time and place of any previously scheduled sale. Lender or its designee may purchase the Property at any sale.

Trustee shall deliver to the purchaser Trustee's deed conveying the Property without any covenant or warranty, expressed or implied. The recitals in the Trustee's deed shall be prima facie evidence of the truth of the statements made therein. Trustee shall apply the proceeds of the sale in the following order: (a) to all expenses of the sale, including, but not limited to, reasonable Trustee's and attorneys' fees; (b) to all sums secured by this Security Instrument; and (c) any excess to the person or persons legally entitled to it.

   23.   **Reconveyance.** Upon payment of all sums secured by this Security Instrument, Lender shall request Trustee to reconvey the Property and shall surrender this Security Instrument and all notes evidencing debt secured by this Security Instrument to Trustee. Trustee shall reconvey the Property without warranty to the person or persons legally entitled to it. Lender may charge such person or persons a reasonable fee for reconveying the Property, but only if the fee is paid to a third party (such as the Trustee) for services rendered and the charging of the fee is permitted under Applicable Law. If the fee charged does not exceed the fee set by Applicable Law, the fee is conclusively presumed to be reasonable.

   24.   **Substitute Trustee.** Lender, at its option, may from time to time appoint a successor trustee to any Trustee appointed hereunder by an instrument executed and acknowledged by Lender and recorded in the office of the Recorder of the county in which the Property is located. The instrument shall contain the name of the original Lender, Trustee and Borrower, the book and page where this Security Instrument is recorded and the name and address of the successor trustee. Without conveyance of the Property, the successor trustee shall succeed to all the title, powers and duties conferred upon the Trustee herein and by Applicable Law. This procedure for substitution of trustee shall govern to the exclusion of all other provisions for substitution.

   25.   **Statement of Obligation Fee.** Lender may collect a fee not to exceed the maximum amount permitted by Applicable Law for furnishing the statement of obligation as provided by Section 2943 of the Civil Code of California.

BY SIGNING BELOW, Borrower accepts and agrees to the terms and covenants contained in this Security Instrument and in any Rider executed by Borrower and recorded with it.

Witnesses:

_____   _____(Seal)
                                                                   - Borrower

_____   _____(Seal)
                                                                   - Borrower

_____[Space Below This Line for Acknowledgment]_____

Promissory Note Secured by Deed of Trust

1. For value received, ☐ I individually ☐ We jointly and severally promise to pay to the order of

   _____

   $_____ at _____

   _____ with interest at the rate of _____% per year: *[choose one]*

   ☐ from the date this note is signed until the date it is due or is paid in full, whichever date occurs last.

   ☐ from the date this note is signed until the date it is paid in full.

2. The signer(s) of this note also agree that this note shall be paid in installments, which include principal and interest, of not less than $_____ per month, due on the first day of each month, until such time as the principal and interest are paid in full.

3. If any installment payment due under this note is not received by the holder within _____ days of its due date, the entire amount of unpaid principal shall become immediately due and payable at the option of the holder without prior notice to the signer(s) of this note.

4. If the holder(s) of this note prevail(s) in a lawsuit to collect on it, the signer(s) agree(s) to pay the holder(s)' attorney fees in an amount the court finds to be just and reasonable.

5. Signer(s) agree(s) that until such time as the principal and interest owed under this note are paid in full, the note shall be secured by a deed of trust to real property commonly known as _____

   _____, owned by _____

   _____ executed on _____ at

   _____ and recorded on

   _____ in the records of _____ County, California.

_____ | _____
Date | Date

_____ | _____
Location (city or county) | Location (city or county)

_____ | _____
Address | Address

_____ | _____

_____ | _____
Signature of Borrower | Signature of Borrower

State of California

County of _____ }

On _____, before me, _____,

a notary public in and for said state, personally appeared _____ personally known to me (or proved to me on the basis of satisfactory evidence) to be the person(s) whose name(s) is/are subscribed to the within instrument, and acknowledged to me that he/she/they executed the same in his/her/their authorized capacity(ies) and that by his/her/their signature(s) on the instrument the person(s), or entity upon behalf of which the person(s) acted, executed the instrument.

[SEAL]

_____
Signature of Notary

Promissory Note Secured by Deed of Trust

1. For value received, ☐ I individually ☐ We jointly and severally promise to pay to the order of

   _____

   $_____ at _____

   _____ with interest at the rate of _____% per year: *[choose one]*

   ☐ from the date this note is signed until the date it is due or is paid in full, whichever date occurs last.

   ☐ from the date this note is signed until the date it is paid in full.

2. The signer(s) of this note also agree that this note shall be paid in installments, which include principal and interest, of not less than $_____ per month, due on the first day of each month, until such time as the principal and interest are paid in full.

3. If any installment payment due under this note is not received by the holder within _____ days of its due date, the entire amount of unpaid principal shall become immediately due and payable at the option of the holder without prior notice to the signer(s) of this note.

4. If the holder(s) of this note prevail(s) in a lawsuit to collect on it, the signer(s) agree(s) to pay the holder(s)' attorney fees in an amount the court finds to be just and reasonable.

5. Signer(s) agree(s) that until such time as the principal and interest owed under this note are paid in full, the note shall be secured by a deed of trust to real property commonly known as _____

   _____, owned by _____

   _____ executed on _____ at

   _____ and recorded on

   _____ in the records of _____ County, California.

Date _____ | Date _____

Location (city or county) _____ | Location (city or county) _____

Address _____ | Address _____

_____ | _____

Signature of Borrower | Signature of Borrower

State of California

County of _____ }

On _____, before me, _____,

a notary public in and for said state, personally appeared _____,

personally known to me (or proved to me on the basis of satisfactory evidence) to be the person(s) whose name(s) is/are subscribed to the within instrument, and acknowledged to me that he/she/they executed the same in his/her/their authorized capacity(ies) and that by his/her/their signature(s) on the instrument the person(s), or entity upon behalf of which the person(s) acted, executed the instrument.

[SEAL]

_____

Signature of Notary

Real Estate Transfer Disclosure Statement

(CALIFORNIA CIVIL CODE § 1102, ET SEQ.)

THIS DISCLOSURE STATEMENT CONCERNS THE REAL PROPERTY SITUATED IN THE CITY OF _____ ,
COUNTY OF _____ , STATE OF CALIFORNIA, DESCRIBED AS _____
_____ .

THIS STATEMENT IS A DISCLOSURE OF THE CONDITION OF THE ABOVE-DESCRIBED PROPERTY IN COMPLIANCE
WITH SECTION 1102 OF THE CIVIL CODE AS OF _____ , _____ . IT IS NOT A WARRANTY
OF ANY KIND BY THE SELLER(S) OR ANY AGENT(S) REPRESENTING ANY PRINCIPAL(S) IN THIS TRANSACTION, AND IT
IS NOT A SUBSTITUTE FOR ANY INSPECTIONS OR WARRANTIES THE PRINCIPAL(S) MAY WISH TO OBTAIN.

I

COORDINATION WITH OTHER DISCLOSURE FORMS

This Real Estate Transfer Disclosure Statement is made pursuant to Section 1102 of the Civil Code. Other statutes require disclosures, depending upon the details of the particular real estate transaction (for example: special study zone and purchase-money liens on residential property).

Substituted Disclosures: The following disclosures and other disclosures required by law, including the Natural Hazard Disclosure Report/Statement that may include airport annoyances, earthquake, fire, flood, or special assessment information, have or will be made in connection with this real estate transfer, and are intended to satisfy the disclosure obligations on this form, where the subject matter is the same:

☐ Inspection reports completed pursuant to the contract of sale or receipt for deposit.

☐ Additional inspection reports or disclosures:

_____ .

(List all substituted disclosure forms to be used in connection with this transaction.)

II

SELLER'S INFORMATION

The Seller discloses the following information with the knowledge that even though this is not a warranty, prospective Buyers may rely on this information in deciding whether and on what terms to purchase the subject property. Seller hereby authorizes any agent(s) representing any principal(s) in this transaction to provide a copy of this statement to any person or entity in connection with any actual or anticipated sale of the property.

THE FOLLOWING ARE REPRESENTATIONS MADE BY THE SELLER(S) AND ARE NOT THE REPRESENTATIONS OF
THE AGENT(S), IF ANY. THIS INFORMATION IS A DISCLOSURE AND IT IS NOT INTENDED TO BE PART OF ANY
CONTRACT BETWEEN THE BUYER AND SELLER.

Seller ☐ is ☐ is not occupying the property.

A. The subject property has the items checked below (read across):

☐ Range	☐ Oven	☐ Microwave
☐ Dishwasher	☐ Trash Compactor	☐ Garbage Disposal
☐ Washer/Dryer Hookups	☐ Rain Gutters	☐ Smoke Detector(s)
☐ Fire Alarm	☐ T.V. Antenna	☐ Satellite Dish
☐ Intercom	☐ Central Heating	☐ Central Air Conditioning
☐ Evaporator Cooler(s)	☐ Wall/Window Air Conditioning	☐ Sprinklers

- ☐ Public Sewer System
- ☐ Septic Tank
- ☐ Sump Pump
- ☐ Water Softener
- ☐ Patio/Decking
- ☐ Built-in Barbecue
- ☐ Sauna
- ☐ Gazebo
- ☐ Burglar Alarms
- ☐ Hot Tub ☐ Locking Safety Cover* ☐ Pool ☐ Child Resistant Barrier* ☐ Spa ☐ Locking Safety Cover*
- ☐ Security Gate(s) ☐ Automatic Garage Door Opener(s)* ☐ # of Remote Controls _____
- ☐ Garage: ☐ Attached ☐ Not Attached ☐ Carport
- ☐ Pool/Spa Heater: ☐ Gas ☐ Solar ☐ Electric
- ☐ Water Heater: ☐ Gas ☐ Water Heater Anchored, Braced, or Strapped* ☐ Electric
- ☐ Water Supply: ☐ City ☐ Well ☐ Private Utility
  - ☐ Other _____
- ☐ Gas Supply: ☐ Utility ☐ Bottled
- ☐ Window Screens ☐ Window Security Bars ☐ Quick Release Mechanism on Bedroom Windows*
- ☐ Exhaust Fan(s) in _____ ☐ 220 Volt Wiring in _____
- ☐ Fireplace(s) in _____ ☐ Gas Starter _____
- ☐ Roof(s): Type: _____ ☐ Age: _____ (approx.)
- ☐ Other: _____

Are there, to the best of your (Seller's) knowledge, any of the above that are not in operating condition?

☐ Yes ☐ No   If yes, then describe. (Attach additional sheets if necessary.)

B. Are you (Seller) aware of any significant defects/malfunctions in any of the following?

☐ Yes ☐ No   If yes, check appropriate box(es) below.

- ☐ Interior Walls
- ☐ Ceilings
- ☐ Floors
- ☐ Exterior Walls
- ☐ Insulation
- ☐ Roof(s)
- ☐ Windows
- ☐ Doors
- ☐ Foundation
- ☐ Slab(s)
- ☐ Driveways
- ☐ Sidewalks
- ☐ Walls/Fences
- ☐ Electrical Systems
- ☐ Plumbing/Sewers/Septics
- ☐ Other Structural Components (describe):

If any of the above is checked, explain. (Attach additional sheets if necessary.) _____

*This garage door opener or child resistant pool barrier may not be in compliance with the safety standards relating to automatic reversing devices as set forth in Chapter 12.5 (commencing with Section 19890) of Part 3 of Division 13, or with the pool safety standards of Article 2.5 (commencing with Section 115920) of Chapter 5 of Part 10 of Division 104, of the Health and Safety Code. The water heater may not be anchored, braced, or strapped in accordance with Section 19211 of the Health and Safety Code. Window security bars may not have quick release mechanisms in compliance with the 1995 Edition of the California Building Standards Code.

C. Are you (Seller) aware of any of the following:

1. Substances, materials, or products that may be an environmental hazard such as, but not limited to, asbestos, formaldehyde, radon gas, lead-based paint, mold, fuel or chemical storage tanks, and contaminated soil or water on the subject property. ☐ Yes ☐ No

2. Features of the property shared in common with adjoining landowners, such as walls, fences, and driveways, whose use or responsibility for maintenance may have an effect on the subject property. ☐ Yes ☐ No

3. Any encroachments, easements, or similar matters that may affect your interest in the subject property. ☐ Yes ☐ No

4. Room additions, structural modifications, or other alterations or repairs made without necessary permits. ☐ Yes ☐ No

5. Room additions, structural modifications, or other alterations or repairs not in compliance with building codes. ☐ Yes ☐ No

6. Fill (compacted or otherwise) on the property or any portion thereof. ☐ Yes ☐ No

7. Any settling from any cause, or slippage, sliding, or other soil problems. ☐ Yes ☐ No

8. Flooding, drainage, or grading problems. ☐ Yes ☐ No

9. Major damage to the property or any other structures from fire, earthquake, floods, or landslides. ☐ Yes ☐ No

10. Any zoning violations, nonconforming uses, or violations of "setback" requirements. ☐ Yes ☐ No

11. Neighborhood noise problems or other nuisances. ☐ Yes ☐ No

12. CC&Rs or other deed restrictions or obligations. ☐ Yes ☐ No

13. Homeowners' association that has any authority over the subject property. ☐ Yes ☐ No

14. Any "common area" (facilities such as pools, tennis courts, walkways, or other areas co-owned in undivided interest with others). ☐ Yes ☐ No

15. Any notices of abatement or citations against the property. ☐ Yes ☐ No

16. Any lawsuits by or against the Seller threatening to or affecting this real property, including any lawsuits alleging a defect or deficiency in this real property or "common areas" (facilities such as pools, tennis courts, walkways, or other areas co-owned in undivided interest with others). ☐ Yes ☐ No

If the answer to any of these is yes, explain (attach additional sheets if necessary): _____

Seller certifies that the information herein is true and correct to the best of the Seller's knowledge as of the date signed by the Seller.

Seller _____ Date _____

Seller _____ Date _____

III

AGENT'S INSPECTION DISCLOSURE (LISTING AGENT)

(To be completed only if the Seller is represented by an agent in this transaction.)

THE UNDERSIGNED, BASED ON THE ABOVE INQUIRY OF THE SELLER(S) AS TO THE CONDITION OF THE PROPERTY AND BASED ON REASONABLY COMPETENT AND DILIGENT VISUAL INSPECTION OF THE ACCESSIBLE AREAS OF THE PROPERTY IN CONJUNCTION WITH THAT INQUIRY, STATES THE FOLLOWING:

☐ Agent notes no items for disclosure.

☐ Agent notes the following items: _____

Agent (Print Name of Broker Representing Seller): _____

By (Associate Licensee or Broker's Signature) _____

Date _____

IV

AGENT'S INSPECTION DISCLOSURE (SELLING AGENT)

(To be completed only if the agent who has obtained the offer is other than the agent above.)

THE UNDERSIGNED, BASED ON A REASONABLY COMPETENT AND DILIGENT VISUAL INSPECTION OF THE ACCESSIBLE AREAS OF THE PROPERTY, STATES THE FOLLOWING:

☐ Agent notes no items for disclosure.

☐ Agent notes the following items: _____

Agent (Print Name of Broker Obtaining Offer) _____

By (Associate Licensee or Broker's Signature) _____

Date _____

V

BUYER(S) AND SELLER(S) MAY WISH TO OBTAIN PROFESSIONAL ADVICE AND/OR INSPECTIONS OF THE PROPERTY AND TO PROVIDE FOR APPROPRIATE PROVISIONS IN A CONTRACT BETWEEN BUYER(S) AND SELLER(S) WITH RESPECT TO ANY ADVICE/INSPECTION/DEFECTS.

I/WE ACKNOWLEDGE RECEIPT OF A COPY OF THIS STATEMENT.

Seller _____ Date _____

Seller _____ Date _____

Buyer _____ Date _____

Buyer _____ Date _____

Agent (Print Name of Broker Representing Seller) _____

By (Associate Licensee or Broker's Signature) _____

Date _____

Agent (Print Name of Broker Obtaining the Offer) _____

By (Associate Licensee or Broker's Signature) _____

Date _____

SECTION 1102.3 OF THE CIVIL CODE PROVIDES A BUYER WITH THE RIGHT TO RESCIND A PURCHASE CONTRACT FOR AT LEAST THREE DAYS AFTER THE DELIVERY OF THIS DISCLOSURE IF DELIVERY OCCURS AFTER THE SIGNING OF AN OFFER TO PURCHASE. IF YOU WISH TO RESCIND THE CONTRACT, YOU MUST ACT WITHIN THE PRESCRIBED PERIOD. A REAL ESTATE BROKER IS QUALIFIED TO ADVISE ON REAL ESTATE. IF YOU DESIRE LEGAL ADVICE, CONSULT YOUR ATTORNEY.

Natural Hazard Disclosure Statement

This statement applies to the following property: _____

The transferor and his or her agent(s) or a third-party consultant disclose the following information with the knowledge that even though this is not a warranty, prospective transferees may rely on this information in deciding whether and on what terms to purchase the subject property. Transferor hereby authorizes any agent(s) representing any principal(s) in this action to provide a copy of this statement to any person or entity in connection with any actual or anticipated sale of the property.

The following are representations made by the transferor and his or her agent(s) based on their knowledge and maps drawn by the state and federal governments. This information is a disclosure and is not intended to be part of any contract between the transferee and transferor.

THIS REAL PROPERTY LIES WITHIN THE FOLLOWING HAZARDOUS AREA(S):

A SPECIAL FLOOD HAZARD AREA (Any type Zone "A" or "V") designated by the Federal Emergency Management Agency.

☐ Yes ☐ No ☐ Do not know and information not available from local jurisdiction

AN AREA OF POTENTIAL FLOODING shown on a dam failure inundation map pursuant to Section 8589.5 of the Government Code.

☐ Yes ☐ No ☐ Do not know and information not available from local jurisdiction

A VERY HIGH FIRE HAZARD SEVERITY ZONE pursuant to Section 51178 or 51179 of the Government Code. The owner of this property is subject to the maintenance requirements of Section 51182 of the Government Code.

☐ Yes ☐ No

A WILDLAND AREA THAT MAY CONTAIN SUBSTANTIAL FOREST FIRE RISKS AND HAZARDS pursuant to Section 4125 of the Public Resources Code. The owner of this property is subject to the maintenance requirements of Section 4291 of the Public Resources Code. Additionally, it is not the state's responsibility to provide fire protection services to any building or structure located within the wildlands unless the Department of Forestry and Fire Protection has entered into a cooperative agreement with a local agency for those purposes pursuant to Section 4142 of the Public Resources Code.

☐ Yes ☐ No

AN EARTHQUAKE FAULT ZONE pursuant to Section 2622 of the Public Resources Code.

☐ Yes ☐ No

A SEISMIC HAZARD ZONE pursuant to Section 2696 of the Public Resources Code.

Landslide Zone ☐ Yes ☐ No ☐ Map not yet released by state
Liquefaction Zone ☐ Yes ☐ No ☐ Map not yet released by state

THESE HAZARDS MAY LIMIT YOUR ABILITY TO DEVELOP THE REAL PROPERTY, TO OBTAIN INSURANCE, OR TO RECEIVE ASSISTANCE AFTER A DISASTER.

THE MAPS ON WHICH THESE DISCLOSURES ARE BASED ESTIMATE WHERE NATURAL HAZARDS EXIST. THEY ARE NOT DEFINITIVE INDICATORS OF WHETHER OR NOT A PROPERTY WILL BE AFFECTED BY A NATURAL DISASTER. BUYER(S) AND SELLER(S) MAY WISH TO OBTAIN PROFESSIONAL ADVICE REGARDING THOSE HAZARDS AND OTHER HAZARDS THAT MAY AFFECT THE PROPERTY.

Signature of Transferor(s):_____ Date: _____

Agent represents that the information herein is true and correct to the best of the agent's knowledge as of the date signed by the agent.

Signature of Agent(s):_____ Date: _____

Signature of Agent(s):_____ Date: _____

Check only one of the following:

☐ Transferor(s) and their agent(s) represent that the information herein is true and correct to the best of their knowledge as of the date signed by the transferor(s) and agent(s).

☐ Transferor(s) and their agent(s) acknowledge that they have exercised good faith in the selection of a third-party report provider as required in Civil Code Section 1103.7, and that the representations made in this Natural Hazard Disclosure Statement are based upon information provided by the independent third-party disclosure provider as a substituted disclosure pursuant to Civil Code Section 1103.4. Neither transferor(s) nor their agent(s) (1) has independently verified the information contained in this statement and report or (2) is personally aware of any errors or inaccuracies in the information contained on the statement. This statement was prepared by the provider below:

Third-Party Disclosure Provider(s) _____ Date _____

Transferee represents that he or she has read and understands this document.

Pursuant to Civil Code Section 1103.8, the representations made in this Natural Hazard Disclosure Statement do not constitute all of the transferor's or agent's disclosure obligations in this transaction.

Signature of Transferee(s) _____ Date _____

Signature of Transferee(s)_____ Date _____

Form for Acknowledgment: Military Personnel

On this the _____ day of _____, _____, before me,

_____, the undersigned

officer, personally appeared _____,

known to me (or satisfactorily proven) to be (a) serving in the armed forces of the United States, (b) a spouse

of a person serving in the armed forces of the United States, or (c) a person serving with, employed by, or

accompanying the armed forces of the United States outside the United States and outside the Canal Zone,

Puerto Rico, Guam, and the Virgin Islands, and to be the person whose name is subscribed to the within

instrument and acknowledged that he executed the same. And the undersigned does further certify that he

is at the date of this certificate a commissioned officer in the active service of the armed forces of the United

States having the general powers of a notary public under the provisions of Section 936 of Title 10 of the

United States Code (Public Law 90-632).

_____
Signature of officer

Serial number

_____
Rank

Branch of service

_____
Capacity in which signed

Declaration of Exemption From Documentary Transfer Tax: Gift of Real Property

Grantor has not received and will not receive consideration from grantee for the transfer made by the attached deed. Therefore, under Revenue and Taxation Code Sec. 11911, the transfer is not subject to the Documentary Transfer Tax.

I declare under penalty of perjury under the laws of California that the foregoing is true and correct.

_____

Grantor

Date: _____ _____, California

_____

Grantor

Date: _____ _____, California

NOLO
www.nolo.com
Declaration of Exemption From Documentary Transfer Tax: Gift of Real Property
Page 1 of 1

Declaration of Exemption From Documentary Transfer Tax: Division of Marital Real Property

The transfer made by the attached deed is made for the purpose of dividing community, quasi-community or quasi-marital real property between spouses, as required by:

☐ a judgment decreeing a dissolution of the marriage or legal separation, by a judgment of nullity, or by any other judgment or order rendered pursuant to Part 5 of Division 4 of the Civil Code, or

☐ a written agreement between the spouses executed in contemplation of such a judgment or order.

Therefore, under Revenue and Taxation Code Sec. 11927, the deed is not subject to the Documentary Transfer Tax.

I declare under penalty of perjury under the laws of California that the foregoing is true and correct.

_____

Grantor

Date: _____ _____, California

_____

Grantor

Date: _____ _____, California

Local Option
Real Estate Transfer Disclosure Statement

THIS DISCLOSURE STATEMENT CONCERNS THE REAL PROPERTY SITUATED IN THE CITY OF _____ _____, COUNTY OF _____, STATE OF CALIFORNIA, DESCRIBED AS _____ _____. THIS STATEMENT IS A DISCLOSURE OF THE CONDITION OF THE ABOVE DESCRIBED PROPERTY IN COMPLIANCE WITH ORDINANCE NO. _____ OF THE _____ CITY OR COUNTY CODE AS OF _____, 20_____. IT IS NOT A WARRANTY OF ANY KIND BY THE SELLER(S) OR ANY AGENT(S) REPRESENTING ANY PRINCIPAL(S) IN THIS TRANSACTION, AND IS NOT A SUBSTITUTE FOR ANY INSPECTIONS OR WARRANTIES THE PRINCIPAL(S) MAY WISH TO OBTAIN.

I

SELLERS' INFORMATION

The seller discloses the following information with the knowledge that even though this is not a warranty, prospective Buyers may rely on this information in deciding whether and on what terms to purchase the subject property. Seller hereby authorizes any agent(s) representing any principal(s) in this transaction to provide a copy of this statement to any person or entity in connection with any actual or anticipated sale of the property.

THE FOLLOWING ARE REPRESENTATIONS MADE BY THE SELLER(S) AS REQUIRED BY THE CITY OR COUNTY OF _____, AND ARE NOT THE REPRESENTATIONS OF THE AGENT(S), IF ANY. THIS INFORMATION IS A DISCLOSURE AND IS NOT INTENDED TO BE PART OF ANY CONTRACT BETWEEN THE BUYER AND SELLER.

1. _____

2. _____

(Example: Adjacent land is zoned for timber production which may be subject to harvest.)

Seller certifies that the information herein is true and correct to the best of the Seller's knowledge as of the date signed by the Seller.

Seller: _____Date: _____

Seller: _____Date: _____

BUYER(S) AND SELLER(S) MAY WISH TO OBTAIN PROFESSIONAL ADVICE AND/OR INSPECTIONS OF THE PROPERTY AND TO PROVIDE FOR APPROPRIATE PROVISIONS IN A CONTRACT BETWEEN BUYER(S) AND SELLER(S) WITH RESPECT TO ANY ADVICE/INSPECTIONS/DEFECTS. I/WE ACKNOWLEDGE RECEIPT OF A COPY OF THIS STATEMENT.

Seller: _____ Date: _____

Seller: _____ Date: _____

Buyer: _____ Date: _____

Buyer: _____ Date: _____

Agent (Broker Representing Seller): _____ Date: _____

By (Associate Licensee or Broker Signature): _____

Agent (Broker Obtaining the Offer): _____ Date: _____

By (Associate Licensee or Broker Signature): _____

A REAL ESTATE BROKER IS QUALIFIED TO ADVISE ON REAL ESTATE. IF YOU DESIRE LEGAL ADVICE, CONSULT YOUR ATTORNEY.

Index

CATALOG

BUSINESS

	PRICE	CODE
Business Buyout Agreements (Book w/CD-ROM)	$49.99	BSAG
The CA Nonprofit Corporation Kit (Binder w/CD-ROM)	$69.99	CNP
California Workers' Comp: How to Take Charge When You're Injured on the Job	$34.99	WORK
The Complete Guide to Buying a Business (Book w/CD-ROM)	$24.99	BUYBU
The Complete Guide to Selling a Business (Book w/CD-ROM)	$24.99	SELBU
Consultant & Independent Contractor Agreements (Book w/CD-ROM)	$29.99	CICA
The Corporate Records Handbook (Book w/CD-ROM)	$69.99	CORMI
Create Your Own Employee Handbook (Book w/CD-ROM)	$49.99	EMHA
Dealing With Problem Employees	$44.99	PROBM
Deduct It! Lower Your Small Business Taxes	$34.99	DEDU
Effective Fundraising for Nonprofits	$24.99	EFFN
The Employer's Legal Handbook	$39.99	EMPL
Essential Guide to Federal Employment Laws	$39.99	FEMP
Form a Partnership (Book W/CD-ROM)	$39.99	PART
Form Your Own Limited Liability Company (Book w/CD-ROM)	$44.99	LIAB
Home Business Tax Deductions: Keep What You Earn	$34.99	DEHB
How to Form a Nonprofit Corporation (Book w/CD-ROM)—National Edition	$49.99	NNP
How to Form a Nonprofit Corporation in California (Book w/CD-ROM)	$49.99	NON
How to Form Your Own California Corporation (Binder w/CD-ROM)	$59.99	CACI
How to Form Your Own California Corporation (Book w/CD-ROM)	$34.99	CCOR
How to Write a Business Plan (Book w/CD-ROM)	$34.99	SBS
Incorporate Your Business (Book w/CD-ROM)	$49.99	NIBS
Investors in Your Backyard (Book w/CD-ROM)	$24.99	FINBUS
The Job Description Handbook	$29.99	JOB
Legal Guide for Starting & Running a Small Business	$34.99	RUNS
Legal Forms for Starting & Running a Small Business (Book w/CD-ROM)	$29.99	RUNSF
LLC or Corporation?	$24.99	CHENT
The Manager's Legal Handbook	$39.99	ELBA
Marketing Without Advertising	$20.00	MWAD
Music Law (Book w/CD-ROM)	$39.99	ML
Negotiate the Best Lease for Your Business	$24.99	LESP
Nolo's Guide to Social Security Disability (Book w/CD-ROM)	$29.99	QSS
Nolo's Quick LLC	$29.99	LLCQ
The Performance Appraisal Handbook	$29.99	PERF
The Small Business Start-up Kit (Book w/CD-ROM)	$24.99	SMBU
The Small Business Start-up Kit for California (Book w/CD-ROM)	$24.99	OPEN
Starting & Running a Successful Newsletter or Magazine	$29.99	MAG
Tax Deductions for Professionals	$34.99	DEPO
Tax Savvy for Small Business	$36.99	SAVVY
Whoops! I'm in Business	$19.99	WHOO
Working for Yourself: Law & Taxes for Independent Contractors, Freelancers & Consultants	$39.99	WAGE
Working With Independent Contractors (Book w/CD-ROM)	$29.99	HICI
Your Crafts Business: A Legal Guide (Book w/CD-ROM)	$26.99	VART
Your Limited Liability Company: An Operating Manual (Book w/CD-ROM)	$49.99	LOP
Your Rights in the Workplace	$29.99	YRW

CONSUMER

	PRICE	CODE
How to Win Your Personal Injury Claim	$29.99	PICL
Nolo's Encyclopedia of Everyday Law	$29.99	EVL
Nolo's Guide to California Law	$24.99	CLAW

Prices subject to change.

	PRICE	CODE
Student & Tourist Visas	$29.99	ISTU
U.S. Immigration Made Easy	$39.99	IMEZ

MONEY MATTERS

	PRICE	CODE
101 Law Forms for Personal Use (Book w/CD-ROM)	$29.99	SPOT
Chapter 13 Bankruptcy: Repay Your Debts	$39.99	CHB
Credit Repair (Book w/CD-ROM)	$24.99	CREP
How to File for Chapter 7 Bankruptcy	$29.99	HFB
IRAs, 401(k)s & Other Retirement Plans: Taking Your Money Out	$34.99	RET
Solve Your Money Troubles	$19.99	MT
Stand Up to the IRS	$29.99	SIRS

PATENTS AND COPYRIGHTS

	PRICE	CODE
All I Need is Money: How to Finance Your Invention	$19.99	FINA
The Copyright Handbook: How to Protect & Use Written Works (Book w/CD-ROM)	$39.99	COHA
Copyright Your Software (Book w/CD-ROM)	$34.95	CYS
Getting Permission: How to License and Clear Copyrighted Materials Online and Off (Book w/CD-ROM)	$34.99	RIPER
How to Make Patent Drawings	$29.99	DRAW
The Inventor's Notebook	$24.99	INOT
Nolo's Patents for Beginners	$24.99	QPAT
Patent, Copyright & Trademark	$39.99	PCTM
Patent It Yourself	$49.99	PAT
Patent Pending in 24 Hours	$34.99	PEND
Patenting Art & Entertainment: New Strategies for Protecting Creative Ideas	$39.99	PATAE
Profit from Your Idea (Book w/CD-ROM)	$34.99	LICE
The Public Domain	$34.99	PUBL
Trademark: Legal Care for Your Business and Product Name	$39.99	TRD
Web and Software Development: A Legal Guide (Book w/ CD-ROM)	$44.99	SFT
What Every Inventor Needs to Know About Business & Taxes (Book w/CD-ROM)	$21.99	ILAX

RESEARCH & REFERENCE

	PRICE	CODE
Legal Research: How to Find & Understand the Law	$39.99	LRES

SENIORS

	PRICE	CODE
Long-Term Care: How to Plan & Pay for It	$19.99	ELD
Social Security, Medicare & Goverment Pensions	$29.99	SOA

SOFTWARE

Call or check our website at www.nolo.com for special discounts on Software!

	PRICE	CODE
Incorporator Pro	89.99	STNC1
LLC Maker—Windows	$89.95	LLP1
Patent Pending Now!	$199.99	PP1
PatentEase—Windows	$349.00	PEAS
Personal RecordKeeper 5.0 CD—Windows	$59.95	RKD5
Quicken Legal Business Pro 2007—Windows	$109.99	SBQB7
Quicken WillMaker Plus 2007—Windows	$79.99	WQP7

SPECIAL UPGRADE OFFER

Save 35% on the latest edition of your Nolo book

Because laws and legal procedures change often, we update our books regularly. To help keep you up-to-date, we are extending this special upgrade offer. Cut out and mail the title portion of the cover of your old Nolo book and we'll give you 35% off the retail price of the New Edition of that book when you purchase directly from Nolo. This offer is to individuals only.

Prices and offer subject to change without notice.

Order Form

Name	
Address	
City	
State, Zip	
Daytime Phone	
E-mail	

Our "No-Hassle" Guarantee

Return anything you buy directly from Nolo for any reason and we'll cheerfully refund your purchase price. No ifs, ands or buts.

☐ Check here if you do not wish to receive mailings from other companies

Item Code	Quantity	Item	Unit Price	Total Price

Method of payment

☐ Check   ☐ VISA

☐ American Express

☐ MasterCard

☐ Discover Card

Subtotal	
Add your local sales tax (California only)	
Shipping: RUSH $12, Basic $9 (See below)	
"I bought 3, ship it to me FREE!" (Ground shipping only)	
TOTAL	

Account Number

Expiration Date

Signature

Shipping and Handling

Rush Delivery—Only $12

We'll ship any order to any street address in the U.S. by UPS 2nd Day Air* for only $12!

* Order by noon Pacific Time and get your order in 2 business days. Orders placed after noon Pacific Time will arrive in 3 business days. P.O. boxes and S.F. Bay Area use basic shipping. Alaska and Hawaii use 2nd Day Air or Priority Mail.

Basic Shipping—$9

Use for P.O. Boxes, Northern California and Ground Service.

Allow 1-2 weeks for delivery.

U.S. addresses only.

For faster service, use your credit card and our toll-free numbers

Call our customer service group Monday thru Friday 7am to 6 pm PST

Phone
1-800-728-3555

Fax
1-800-645-0895

Mail
Nolo
950 Parker St.
Berkeley, CA 94710

NOLO

Order 24 hours a day @ www.nolo.com

Get the Latest in the Law

Nolo's Legal Updater
We'll send you an email whenever a new edition of your book is published! Sign up at **www.nolo.com/legalupdater**.

Updates at Nolo.com
Check **www.nolo.com/update** to find recent changes in the law that affect the current edition of your book.

Nolo Customer Service
To make sure that this edition of the book is the most recent one, call us at **800-728-3555** and ask one of our friendly customer service representatives (7:00 am to 6:00 pm PST, weekdays only). Or find out at **www.nolo.com**.

Complete the Registration & Comment Card ...
... and we'll do the work for you! Just indicate your preferences below:

- -

Registration & Comment Card

NAME _____ DATE _____

ADDRESS _____

CITY _____ STATE _____ ZIP _____

PHONE _____ EMAIL _____

COMMENTS _____

WAS THIS BOOK EASY TO USE?   (VERY EASY)   5   4   3   2   1   (VERY DIFFICULT)

☐ Yes, you can quote me in future Nolo promotional materials. *Please include phone number above.*

☐ Yes, send me **Nolo's Legal Updater** via email when a new edition of this book is available.

Yes, I want to sign up for the following email newsletters:

    ☐ **NoloBriefs** (monthly)
    ☐ **Nolo's Special Offer** (monthly)
    ☐ **Nolo's BizBriefs** (monthly)
    ☐ **Every Landlord's Quarterly** (four times a year)

☐ Yes, you can give my contact info to carefully selected partners whose products may be of interest to me.

NOLO

DEED 7

Nolo
950 Parker Street
Berkeley, CA 94710-9867
www.nolo.com

YOUR LEGAL COMPANION